Historical Model Railway Society

HMRS Livery Register no.3

LSWR and Southern

By L. Tavender

Contents

Acknowledgments

The compilation of this book has only been possible because of the willing help given by a large number of people. I wish to thank all of them for that help, which they gave sometimes without knowing it. May I thank, too, the unrecorded contributors, especially those who took part in the early stages of the project. Special help has been given by: Mr. J. Scholes, Curator of Historical Relics, British Railways Board, and his staff at the Museum of British Transport, Clapham; Mr. E. Fowkes, the British Railways Archivist; Miss M. MacFarlane, lately Curator of the Willis Museum, Basingstoke; Mr. P. S. Peberdy, Curator of the City of Southampton Museums Department; the Trustees and Council of the Dorset County Museum, Dorchester; Mr. H. Ward, British Railways Area Manager, Bournemouth; Mr. D. E. Eddowes, Editor of the *Paint, Oil and Colour Journal*; Mr. A. R. Brown, Editor of the *Railway Observer*; the staffs of the Public Libraries at Poole and Bournemouth; the Hampshire Narrow Gauge Railway Society; Mr. J. Geach, Secretary of the Model Railway Club.

Mr. J. T. Howard Turner, lately Chairman of the HMRS, kindly prepared the manuscript of which Section 7 is but a slight enlargement. Mr. H. V. Tumilty has given extensive help over a long period in this project, and without his close study, for the HMRS, of the photographic evidence and the BTHR Archives, and his acquisition of paint fragments, the narrative could not have been put together at all. The specialist in the subject for the South Western Circle, Mr. C. J. Peacock, has also devoted much time to the project, and also searched for old paint. Together with him, Mr. R. Meredith has searched the printed literature. The information on S R rolling stock derives mainly from Mr. R. Chorley's study of the Eastleigh drawings, and that on S R locomotives has in great part been the work of Messrs. A. Sedgwick, J. Fairman, B. I. Fletcher and D. L. Bradley. The drawings of the name and number plates are the work of Messrs. H. A. Shelley and (the greater part) T. Adcock, while the decorations on pp. 4 and 29 are drawn from potsherds discovered on the site of the Bentley and Bordon branch by C. J. and J. Peacock respectively.

The contributions of the following people (who, in common with those in the foregoing list are by no means all members of the HMRS) have been many and various; where practicable, acknowledgment has been made in the text: N. L. Abbott, T. Adcock, T. Barfoot, P. E. Barnes, I. D. Beale, M. Bishop, B. Bigwood, A. Blackburn, A. Brackenborough, D. Burton, P. Chatham, B. W. O. Chicken, J. J. Davis, S. B. Dent, C. H. Ellis, D. K. Fritz, H. Girod-Eymery, F. C. Hambleton, W. J. Hughes, D W. Knight, J. W. Knowles, A. B. Macleod, D. McCann, H. Morgan, K. O'B. Nichols, M. Palmer, J. F. Parker, N. Pattenden, G. H. Platt, R. R. Potts, I. J. Pusey, M. Rhodes, J. Rowland, G. A. Russell, J. H. C. Sadler, H. A. Shelley, P. Tatlow, R. E. Tustin, J. Watling, A. J. Wallace, J. Wallis, A. Werge-Hartley, D. Wigley, Beti Williams, Janet Woolgar.

Mr. George Dow and Mr. J. T. Howard Turner have kindly read the various sections in proof and made a number of useful additions and criticisms. I am grateful to Mr. K. Hill, Pamela A. Holmes, Mr. R. Meredith and Margaret Turkington for willing help with the typing of the manuscript under very trying conditions, many of which were my fault. The same qualification applies to the process of putting the text into print and I am grateful to Mr.Norman Wilkinson of Fraser Meikle Ltd. for his forbearance. Finally, I wish to acknowledge the parts played by Mr. A. E. West, formerly Secretary of the South Western Circle, whose agitations really set this book in train, and by Mr. S. R. Arnold, also of the South Western Circle, by his staunch insistence on the need to "go and have a look"

L.T.

Published by
The Historical Model Railway Society
59 Woodberry Way, Chingford, London, E4 7DY

SBN: 902835 00 9
and printed in Great Britain by
Wembley Press Ltd., Reading

Section 1 Notes on the use of this book

1.1 The L S W R did not hold the record for frequency of changing its liveries, but the writer is quite content that such a dubious claim to fame should rest with another company, and perhaps the long-suffering painters at Nine Elms sixty-odd years ago would have agreed. If one keeps to basics, however, there were only two main liveries after the fluid state of the years before 1850. From 1850 to 1883 everything was brown, and from then on the engines were green. From just before the grouping in 1923, the carriages were green also. All the rest was but detail, in spite of the arguments which have taken place since.

In the following pages, the successive liveries of each main category of railway equipment are described as continuous stories running from as near 1839 as the evidence permits, down to the nationalisation of the Southern Railway at New Year, 1948.

In describing liveries, there are two main problems to be solved. The lesser is the description of where the different colours were applied. The greater is the definition of the colour shades themselves. In the absence of the comprehensive series of paint specimens which are available, for instance, for the Great Western Railway, recourse has been made to many other sources, including verbal descriptions, some of which are obviously the product of a struggle to find an apt phrase. It is clear that many references are not original sources but unattributed quotations, and it is a minor hazard of research to find the same information reappearing like some Cheshire cat in yet another place. The writer has to admit that in many cases he has only been able to turn the cat on again. Where a reliable sample is available, a standard designation and reference is given according to a daylight visual comparison with a standard colour chart, usually the Nickerson colour fan[1] published by the Munsell Color Co., but in some cases one of the other colour charts listed below has been used [2-9]. The standard form of a reference to an actual sample of the paint in question is as follows: e.g.

Dark brownish gray 2·5 YR 2/2

In the case of such secondary sources as a published colour plate or a model, the reference is given in brackets, thus:

(Dark brownish gray 2·5 YR 2/2)

When an exact match was not found, the word (near) has been added; when a Munsell value has been estimated with reference to the colour fan, the abbreviation "est." has been added.

Because the colour names used in British charts are not systematic (and some charts do not name colours), other colour names listed in this book are those allocated by the (U.S.A.) National Bureau of Standards [10] to correspond to the given Munsell references. American spellings have been retained.

Colour designations which have been found to have been in use by the railways themselves are printed in *italics*. Usually, one colour description is also given in **bold** type. This is the one which the writer feels is the most representative for modelling purposes.

1.2 Inconsistency of colours.

During the preparation of this book, it was confirmed that surviving paint samples and fragments of a given nominal colour varied widely in shade, a discovery which accounted in part for the variety of descriptions to be found in print. As most of the samples were examined after the removal of any layer which had been exposed to the atmosphere, it is felt that the observed variations reflect actual inconsistencies in the original paint colours. This is an additional reason for giving numerous colour references, and diagrams have been prepared to help readers to visualise the variations which have been found to occur. I have tried not to get drawn into ill-informed speculation on the indeterminable effects of rain, sunlight or chemical attack, if only because I am not qualified to write of such matters, but unless there is a note to the contrary it may be assumed that the colours are free from dirt and varnish. Also, a set of colour patches is given in Appendix 4 and references to British Standard or other colours of which accurate patterns can be obtained at moderate prices have been added in the text.

For a full explanation of the Munsell colour reference system, the reader must go to textbooks [11-13], but for our purpose we can say that the Munsell system defines colours by a position reference in a hypothetical solid in a manner analogous to geographical longitude and latitude. Longitude is represented by a group of letters, in order R, YR, Y, GY, G. BG, B, PB, P, RP, which denote the colours of the spectrum starting at red and proceeding around the circle through yellow, green and blue to red again. Prefix numbers 2·5, 5, 7·5 and 10 give 40 hue divisions as present on the fan referred to in section 1.1. Latitude is represented by a figure ranging from 0 (= black, at the "south pole") to 10 (= white, at the "north pole"). Following this "value" figure is a number such as /5. This figure represents the "chroma", or roughly speaking the intensity, of the colour and is notionally measured at right angles to the line joining the "north and south poles". Colours which are close to white or black are clearly not very intense, and so the "colour solid" is roughly spherical, with pronounced bulges in the orange and mauve neighbourhoods. To help in visualising the relation between observed colour shades, a chart is given in Appendix 3 in which Munsell references are plotted as a grid of hue versus value (chroma is indicated by the dash figure adjacent to the black spot).

References to sources of information are denoted by figures in square brackets and are printed at the end of each section of this book.

References

The following colour standards have been found useful in the compilation of this book:

1. *Nickerson color fan, maximum chroma, 40 hues,* published by the Munsell Color Co., Inc., Baltimore, Md., U.S.A., for which the British agents are Messrs. Tintometer Ltd., Salisbury.
2. *British Standard 381C : 1930 Colours for ready mixed paints* (obsolete).
3. ,, ,, *381C : 1948 Colours for ready mixed paints* (obsolete).
4. ,, ,, *381C : 1964 Colours for specific purposes.*
5. ,, ,, *2660 : 1955 Colours for building and decorative paints.*
6. *British Colour Council Dictionary of colour standards,* adopted by the British Standards Institution as *BS 543 : 1934.* London, British Colour Council, 1934 (obsolete).
7. *Dictionary of colours for interior decoration.* London, British Colour Council, 1949, 3 vols.
8. *Munsell Color Atlas and Book of Color* (U.S.A.). Details are omitted since this work is expensive and is obtainable only with great difficulty through the Public Library System in the U.K.
9. Carter, E. F., *Britain's Railway Liveries . . . 1825-1948, London,* Harold Starke, 1963, colour chart.
10. *The I S C C-N B S Method of Designating Colors and a Dictionary of Color Names* (N B S Circular no. 553), Washington, D.C., U.S. Government Printing Office, 1955, pp. 16-31. Not easily obtained in the U.K.; copy available via HMRS Library.
11. *Encyclopaedia Britannica.*
12. Taylor, C. J. A. and Marks, S. (Eds.), *Paint Technology Manuals, pt. 6 : Pigments, Dyestuffs and Lakes,* London, Chapman and Hall for the Oil and Colour Chemists' Association, 1966, pp. 58-61.
13. Hayman, R., 'Systems of Colour Classification' in *Amateur Photographer,* v. 139, no. 5, p. 64 (6th Aug. 1969).

Section 2 **Locomotives**

2.1 L S W R locomotives 1839-50.

Passenger locomotives were dark ("bottle") green, lined out with fine red and white lines [1] and apparently unlettered [2]. Goods engines were painted black with red lining and wheels [1]. Numbers were applied in gold on the front buffer beams and tender backs [1].

2.2 1843(?)-60.

The dating of this scheme is doubtful and the descriptions of the colours contradictory in the sources available.

Colour:

A: Indian red [3]
Dark Indian red [4, 5, 6]
Chocolate [7]
Venetian red (given by Ellis for J. Beattie's earliest engines) [8]
Strong reddish brown, no. 445 of BS 381C:1964 10 R 3/8 (near) [9, 10]
Deep crimson [11]
Crimson [12]
Indian red, the colour of which varied somewhat [13]
Enriched Indian red [14]

The upper works and wheels were colour A; the smokebox, chimney, boiler bands, springs, axleboxes and brake-blocks were black. The lining consisted of black bands edged in white (or possibly yellow [7]) (fig. 1a) with vermilion edges to the splasher slots. Lining was often omitted in repainting [1], or plain black bands used [14]. Older engines were unlined black [1].

2.3 1865-7 [13] (but Ellis gives this period as c. 1859 to the early 1870s [5]).

In this period, some information can be deduced from photographs and a colour plate was published long ago [15].

Colour:

A: **Deep reddish brown, no. 452 of BS 381C: 1964 7·5 R 2/6** [10]
Dark brown [16]
Chocolate [13]
Rich chocolate [3]
Deep rich umber brown [14]
Dull red [17]

B: Vermilion [14]

The boiler, cab, splashers, side tanks, bunker, outside frames (exterior), valances, outside cylinders, footsteps, all engine wheels, tender body, frames and axleboxes, and ends of buffer beams were colour A. The interior of frames [16], buffer beams [13], buffer casings and also, initially, the exterior of the outside frames [3] (but not the cranks) of the Beyer, Peacock 0-6-0 engines were vermilion [13, 18]. Smokeboxes and their doors and feedwater exhaust pipes were black. (The practice of painting frames red, so common in the 19th century, was a natural carry-over from the wheelwrights' tradition and possibly reflects an ancient concern with the dangers of unfenced machinery).

Lining was carried out on splashers, sandboxes, side tanks, bunkers, outside cylinders and tender sides (where it was laid out in three panels). The bands (fig. 1b) consisted of a black stripe, edged on the inside with white and on the outside with colour B [13, 14, 16]. According to Ellis [6, 8], the vermilion lining was only carried by the best express engines, and the ordinary lining was white and black only. This is confirmed by Mr. Kerley [19]. Similiar lining was applied to the splasher slots, in which case the vermilion line, when present, was furthest from the edge of the slot [19]. Boiler bands were black with white edges [3, 20] (fig. 1k1), sometimes elaborated with red lines (fig. 1k2 [21]), and similar lining was applied to sandbox fronts and tender axleboxes. Valances may have been lined either in colour B and white [16, 19] or have had a black edge with a line of colour B bordering the brown [16] (fig. 1f). Buffer beams had a white line and a black edge; the ends were lined as the panels of the engine [5, 13, 16]. The usual parts (outside motion, buffer heads, pipework on the engine, handrails and also occasionally the smokebox door edge) were left bright. Engine numbers were carried in gilt figures on the boiler side, and in the form "N°/123" on the buffer beam (but at the front only?). The latter were shaded black [13, 16]. Hearsay suggests that the flywheels of feed-pumps were painted red with polished rims [21].

A curiosity was the habit of polishing iron domes, safety-valve covers and smokebox door rims [12], which naturally rusted almost immediately, and the practice lingered until 1881 of painting chimney caps in vermilion, orange or salmon to simulate polished metal [13] — the observation of no. 81 *Herod* at Waterloo in this period as being painted purple [3, 22] is surely an example of this rather than a special paint scheme for a funeral train (incidentally, *Herod* must at the time have been fairly near the end of its service life).

2.4 Passenger and possibly goods locomotives in the seventies (July 1872 to late 1879 [23]).

Colours:

A: Dark brown (a paler chocolate than that used previously and known as *purple brown*) [23]
Deep rich umber brown [10, 14]

B: Yellow ochre [3, 23]
Deep yellow [14]

The boiler, dome, splashers and cab sheets were dark brown [19]. The smokebox and chimney were black [19]. Lining was carried out in ochre, edged on both sides by a fine white line [3, 14, 23] (fig. 1c). Mr. Kerley gives the general lining as white with the yellow/white combination on the boiler bands and splashers [19]. Exeter shops were using up the darker chocolate paint at this time [23].

2.5 The Adams brown livery: 1879 [23, 24] to 1884 [25, 26]

Colours:

A: Umber [3, 23, 27]
Raw umber [24]
Dark umber [24]
Brown [25, 28]
Chocolate brown [26]
Dull yellow-brown [17]
. . . rather dull brown tint [29]
Darker, fresher looking brown [30]

B: Vermilion [27]
Orange [3, 12, 14]

C: Light green [24]
Bright green [3, 12, 24]
Pea green [14, 31]

The basic brown colour was changed to umber from the latter half of 1879, the first classes affected being the 46 and 380 classes delivered then [23]. The lining too was altered, the cab, tender and splasher panels being edged in black, with a fine green line dividing it from the brown and a further pair of lines — narrow orange outside fine green — being set about an inch within the brown (fig. 1d1) [23]. Boiler bands were black, with white (or green? [27]) edges and fine orange lines about half an inch away on the boiler cladding (fig. 1.1) [23]. Outside cylinders were edged in black and lined in orange [32], wheel centres were lined in orange at hub and rim [32] and spring buckles were lined orange. The 46 and 380 class tank engines ("Ironclad") had cast crests above the numbers on the tanks [23], but in 1878-9 the "Metropolitan" class 4-4-0Ts and 135 class 4-4-0s were decorated with painted (or transfer) coats of arms below the numerals and on the tender sides respectively [33] (cf. contemporary coach livery in Section 3.5). In 1879-80 some Exeter repaints in the old dark chocolate colour were put into traffic with purple chimney caps [23]. The foregoing scheme was in effect when the specification was issued for the first 4-4-2T engines in June 1884, and from that document [25] the following details are quoted:

> *Painting*. Before any paint is applied, the ironwork must be cleaned and free from scales and rust. The boiler is to receive two coats of red oxide paint before being lagged. The outside of boiler clothing plates, frames, cylinders, wheels, outside of hand-rail plate and cab are to have one coat of lead colour, two coats of filling up, stopped with hard stopping, then to be rubbed down, followed by two coats of lead colour, faced with pumice-stone between, after which two coats of brown colour to pattern.
> The picking out and fine lining are to be to pattern panel which will be supplied by this Company. The smoke-box, chimney, back of firebox, ash pan, footplate, brake work and side springs are to have one coat of lead colour and two coats of Japan black. The inside of frames and cross stays are to have two coats of red oxide paint. Front of buffer plates, life guards, buffer casings and inside of cab are to be painted vermilion.
> The axles are to have two coats of white lead.
> All the painting on the outside of the engine is to have three coats of best hard-drying body varnish. All paint on the inside of the engine is to have one coat of best hard-drying body varnish. All varnish is to be of the best quality, and to sample . . .
> *Quality* . . . The number of the engine is to be figured in gilt numbers on front and hind buffer plates, and in solid brass figures on the hand-rail plate on each side of the engine. Samples of the gilt numbers and patterns of the brass figures will be supplied by the Company . . .
> *General Mountings*. Four lamp irons at front of engine to this Company's pattern, three fixed on front of smoke-box and one on back of buffer-plate, and four lamp irons on back of tank to this Company's pattern.

The choice of vermilion for the cab interior seems very curious, in view of the knowledge that is believed to have been available in the 19th century about the desirability of having restful and non-distracting colours in front of enginemen. This and some other features of the livery seem to have been recalled by the maker of a notable model of an L S W R locomotive of a somewhat later date [34].

A minor structural point: the square cab windows characteristic of Adams' engines had varnished mahogany frames [35].

2.6 Goods locomotives 1883-1922, and secondary passenger locomotives 1883-7 [36].

(Burtt gives "about the 1885 period" [29], Ahrons gives the date as "about 1886" [17], while Bushell [26] states that he saw one of the Adams 4-4-2Ts in this livery in 1884 (cf. Section 2.5).

This scheme, developed by Adams in 1883, appears to have continued in use until the grouping with such little modification that it needs to be considered as a continuous topic.

Colours:

A: Dark green [17, 27, 28]
Dark bronze green [14]
Holly green [12, 37]
Dark holly green [3]
Black or very dark green [38]
Very dark green, almost black [10, 39]
Very dark green, no. 6-068 of BS 2660:1955
5 G 2/2 [40] ★ 4

B: Bright green [24, 37]
Light green [3, 12, 14]
Moderate yellowish green, no. 6-072 of BS 2660:1955
10 GY 6/4 [40]

As originally specified, the boiler, main frames (below the platform), safety valve lever, outside cylinders, valances, footsteps, wheel centres, tender frames, hornplates, springs, hangers, outside cranks, coal coping and the front of axleboxes were painted dark green [41]. Bogie frames and tender axleboxes were black, and guard irons, buffer sockets and buffer beams were vermilion [41]. Lining was carried out on the boiler bands, cab panels, splashers, sand boxes, cylinder clothing, footsteps and tender sides and end, all of which were edged in black and lined in light green (fig.

5a). The edge of the coal coping was black, unlined [41]. No lettering was carried at first, the engine number was marked by cut-out brass figures on the cab side, with the usual presentation on the buffer beams. Other, later, details of lettering and shape of lining conformed to contemporary passenger-engine practice. Long before Urie's time, the guard irons, and probably the frames too had become black.

Cab interiors were buff and the frame interiors (with the motion plate) were probably tan. Toolboxes on the engine platform (eg. on Beattie 2-4-0Ts) were painted as for tanks. The following parts of engines were painted black [42]: cab roof exterior, splasher and tank tops, tank ends, outside motion plate, outside cylinder ends, step treads, guard irons, axles, axle ends, tyres, tender interior, coal rails, hornplates, axleboxes, springs, spring hangers, brake gear, toolboxes on tender platforms and top. As before, buffer beams were vermilion and motion, buffer heads and handrails bright. Builders' plates were retained, but no coats of arms were carried.

2.7 Adams' passenger engine livery, 1885-95.

The dark green livery seems to have been an early stage in a search for a durable finish. Adams experimented with a pea green livery, at first on locomotive nos. 142 and 448-9. After inspection of these by the Directors on 22nd July 1885 [37], Adams was authorised, on 5th August, to introduce the pea green scheme as standard [43], the dark green livery being retained for secondary engines. Presumably between 1883 and 1885 a good number of the principal engines were also painted dark green. There are references in print to the introduction of both the dark and light green schemes in 1872+ and 1877 or '79 [38, 44], but these are not supported by evidence and it is felt that they are probably inaccurate recollections. Later, on 28th August 1885, Adams was able to report that the Nine Elms paint shops had turned out 42 engines in the (presumably light) green livery [45].

Colours:

A: Light green [14, 17, 28, 44]
Pea green [3. 12, 36]
Fresh bright-looking green [30]
Grass green [46]
(Moderate olive green, no. 5-065 of BS 2660: 1955 — 5 GY 4/6 [34])
Moderate olive green — 7·5 GY 4/4 [47] ★1
(Moderate yellow green, Carter's no. 2 — 7·5 GY 5/7 [48])
(Moderate yellow green, no. 6-071 of BS 2660: 1955 — 7·5 GY 7/4 [49])
(Moderate olive green — 7·5 GY 4/4 [50])
(Strong yellow green — 5 GY 7/10 to 7·5 GY 6/8 [51])

B: *Torbay red oxide* — Appendix 1.2
(Possibly moderate reddish brown, no. 1-018 of BS 2660:1955 — 7·5 R 3/4 [34])

C: *Tan* [52]
Dark orange yellow, no. 359 of BS 381C: 1964 — 10 YR 6·5/8 or
no. 360 — 7·5 YR 5·5/6 [10]

D: *Vermilion* [52]
(Vivid red, no. 537 of BS 381C:1964 — 7·5 R 4·5/16 [34])

One of Adams' specifications survives in print [52] and was as follows:

SPECIFICATION OF FOUR WHEELS COUPLED BOGIE PASSENGER ENGINE . . .

Painting. Before any paint is applied, the iron work must be cleaned and be free from scales and rust. The boiler is to receive one coat of boiled oil while warm, and two coats of Torbay red oxide paint before being lagged. The inside of the clothing to receive one coat of red oxide. The outside of the clothing plates, wheels, the sides and front of cab, the sides of splashers to have one coat of lead colour, two coats of filling up, stopped with hard stopping, then rubbed down, followed by two coats of lead colour faced with pumice stone between, after which two coats of light green to pattern. The picking out and fine lining are to be to pattern panel, which will be supplied by the Company. The outside of frames, guard bars, tops of splashers, smokebox, chimney, back of firebox, ashpan, footplate, brake work and side springs are to have one coat of lead colour paint and two coats of Japan black. The inside of frames and cross-stays to have one coat of Torbay red oxide and one coat of tan colour to pattern. Front of buffer plates and buffer casing to be painted vermilion; inside of cab to have one coat of lead colour, two coats of filling up, and two coats of tan colour to pattern. The axles are to have one coat of lead colour and one coat of Japan black. All the painting on the outside of the engine to have three coats of the best engine copal varnish of the very best quality, and flatted between the coats.

SPECIFICATION OF SIX WHEELS TENDER.

Painting. Before any paint is applied, the iron work must be clean and free from scale or rust. The inside of the tank is to have two good coats of thick red-lead paint, the outside being prepared and finished in a similar manner to the engine. The top and bottom of the tank, footplate and brake work are to have one coat of lead-colour paint, and one coat of Japan black.

The gilt numbers are to be put on the tender buffer plate, and letters on sides according to instructions and samples which will be supplied, and all the iron work is to be stamped with the Company's initials.

Elsewhere [53], it was specified that the black parts were to include the tank tops and ends, axleboxes, spring buckles, hangers and the ends of Westinghouse reservoirs — the general paint scheme being as above. The cab roof and its rear, curved angle iron were black [54, 55]. The interior of the cab was buff, colour C, now [53], instead of the psychologically irritating and unsafe red, and compared with the earlier specification printed in Section 2.5 the only other noteworthy change was the substitution of tan for red inside the frames. Possibly the brown paint stood up to lubricants without varnish and was thus more economical. The change to black axles probably reflects a reduced fear of their cracking [56], but the date of manufacture continued to be stamped on the axle ends [57].

The lining on the cab front and sides (often in two panels there — see fig. 4b [54]), on splasher sides, tender sides and end, cylinder clothing, Westinghouse reservoir (where it formed a panel) and pump, consisted of a black edge with a thin ($\frac{3}{16}$ in. [55]) white line. The panels had corners with radii of up to 3 in. [55], and the black edging was likewise three inches wide where possible, but in restricted places such as the bottom of the splashers it was reduced to 1½ in. and where account had to be taken of brass splasher edging the width of the black line was reduced to as little as 1 inch [55]. The treatment of the junction between cab front and splasher was such that the green was continued down over the curve of the splasher as far as the lowest point of the dip between the wheel arches. There it terminated at a transverse line forward of which the splasher top was black [55].

Although a few 4-4-0s were turned out in 1885 with a monogram (fig. 2b [58]) on the front splashers — an obvious copy of the current G W R insignia — in general no company identification was carried until 1887 when the letters L & S W R appeared on tank or tender sides, together with the new brass number plates [37]. Soon the inscription was altered to L S W R [37], as before being in gilt letters shaded black. The letters were spaced in different ways, but seemingly at rational intervals (figs. 4a, b [59]), and were generally placed a little higher than half-way up the tender panel [46], with a tendency, especially on tank engines, to align the tops of the letters with the tops of the figures in the number plate [59]. The precise form of the letters and shading varied a little; fig. 2a is taken from a late Nine Elms drawing [54]; the spacing of the letters is confirmed by a second original drawing [60]. These two drawings also show omission of the picking out and lining from the footstep plate where it abutted the drag-beam, and from the angle-iron between cab front and boiler cladding; but the works painters seem to have done these parts on their own initiative [59]. At this late period too (1893), a simplified monogram (fig. 2d [55]) was brought into use; the older version had apparently been in use right up to then.

The elliptical number plates (fig. 3a [61]) were strictly of Stratford G E R pattern [62] and had red grounds [46, 63]. Adams had special plates cast for many Beattie engines duplicated from 1887 onwards [37], (fig. 3b [64]). In addition to these plates, earlier plates were retained. Duplication of engines by adding a zero prefix to the number was effected without regard to the symmetry of the numbers on either side of the cab [59].

The engine number was displayed on the front buffer beam using gilt numerals of much the same form as later. The loops of the figures were more regular and the shading had slightly concave diagonal edges [55]. The height of the figures was 4½ in. [55], with an addition of ¾ in. black shading (fig. 2c) [55].

We may at this point notice the entry in the Locomotive Committee minutes on 9th June 1886 [65], which refers to a discussion on whether a uniform colour could be adopted for all the Company's stock. At this date, it is likely that locomotives could be seen in umber, dark green and light green finishes, and coaches in salmon, umber and dark green too (see Section 3.7). Perhaps this incident was the occasion for the extension of the light green livery to all passenger engines in April 1887 [37].

2.8 Drummond's experimental yellow livery, 1897 [37, 66, 67]

The reason for Drummond's trial of a yellow livery is not apparent, but it might have been a result either of nostalgia for his younger days at Inverness and Brighton works, or perhaps of an antipathy to paints including blue pigments. The locomotive concerned, T7 4-2-2-0 no. 720, was neatly painted in what was in effect the Adams style with the substitution of yellow for green with black picking out (i.e. bordering) and white lining. But the latter had squared-off corners instead of the radii used by Adams. However, close examination of the official photograph suggests that the white lining may have been bounded on the outside by a black or red line, with the outer margin of the panels in some other dark colour. The lettering on the tender was also unusual: the letters L S W in approximate 9 in. block capitals — probably gilt with black shading. These were evenly spaced so as to divide the length of the panel into four, but their centres were about an inch above the half height of the yellow rectangle. This engine is also said to have been known as the "blue elephant", and this name has prompted further speculation on whether it bore a different coloured livery [68].

2.9 The Drummond passenger engine livery, 1895-Oct. 1917 [37].

Drummond's standard scheme followed closely, as to lining and layout, the liveries employed by him on the North British [69] and Caledonian Railways [70] in 1875-82 and 1883-91 respectively. The general scheme survived into Urie's time — it appears still to have been common until late in 1920 [71] — but the shades of colour have been a matter of great dispute, as can be seen from the descriptions printed in the table which follows. The first Drummond green, here designated A1, appears not to have been the same as the preceding Adams green, being a little yellower and more intense. However, many writers (Ahrons [17], Twining [14], Thompson [28], Walker [30] and Hambleton [69]) say or imply that the Adams and Drummond colours were the same — Ahrons, Thompson and Walker in fact state that the Adams colour lasted until the grouping. But Bradley [37] does distinguish between the shades used by the two engineers, and further says that a new colour, sage green, was introduced in December 1914 [72].

Colours:

A1: *Royal green* [37], alternatively *Tartan green* [37] or *Engine green* [72]

Appendix 1.3 and 1.4

Green, very like . . . young grass in spring [73]
Apple green [37]
Bright green [74]
Very bright yellow-green [40]
Fresh bright-looking green [30]
Light green [17, 28, 75]
Light green, growing yellower in tinge as the present century advanced [5]
Moderate yellow green
5 GY 5/6 [76]
(Moderate olive green
5 GY 4/3 [77])
(Moderate olive green
5 GY 4·5/6 est. [78]) ★2

(Moderate yellow green
5 GY 5/6 [79])
(Strong yellow green, Carter's no. 17
6 GY 6/8 est. [48])
(Strong yellow green 7·5 GY 5/7 approx. [80])
(Strong yellow green 7·5 GY 6/8 [81])
(Moderate yellowish green
10 GY 5/6 [82])

A2: Less bright yellow-green, more apple green [40]
Lightish olive [83]
Pale olive green [84]
(Moderate olive green
2·5 GY 4/3 [85])
(Moderate yellow green, no. 278 of BS 381C: 1964 (near) 5 GY 5·5/4 [85])

A3: *Sage green* [72] Appendix 1.3
Green considerably darkened [63]
(Dark yellowish green, Carter's no. 10
10 GY 4/6 est. [48])
The apparent similarity of this colour to sage green used in 1917-22 is discussed in Section 2.10.

B1: *Purple brown* Appendix 1.5
Brown [63]
Light brown [57]
Chocolate [5, 72, 75, 86]
Purplish brown [10, 74]
Cardinal red . . . a dull red [87]
Indian red [14]
Very deep red, no. 1-019 of BS 2660:1955
7·5 R 2/8 [40]
(Dark brown, no. 412 of BS 381C:1964
5 YR 2/4 [78]) ★ 8
(Dark red 5 R 3/7 [80, 82])
(Dark reddish brown, no. 449 of BS 381C: 1964 7·5 R 2/4 [81])
(Moderate reddish brown
7·5 R 3/6 [77])

B2: (Moderate reddish brown
10 R 3/4 [85])
(Strong brown, no. 489 of BS 381C: 1964
5 YR 3·5/6 (near) [85])

C: *Vermilion* [88]

D: Gilt [75, 89]

E: **Oak grain** [88]
Grained [75]
Light golden brown [90]
Yellow [91]
Dark brown [40]
Stone [92]

F: **Tan** [88]
Bright brown [93]

The boiler, firebox water tube covers, the lever, casing and base of Ramsbottom safety valves, dome, valances, outside cylinders, footsteps, all wheel bosses, cranks, spokes and rims, tender sides and end, cab front and sides, (and probably usually the back of the cab of tank engines [59]), splasher sides, sandbox, tank and bunker sides, bunker ends, frame exteriors of six-wheel tenders, Westinghouse pump and reservoir [42] and the coal panel of Urie H15 class 4-6-0s were all painted green [77]. The subsidiary colour B was applied to the front of combined sandboxes and splashers, front of tanks [59], coal flare, outside frames of bogie tenders [77], toolboxes on tender platforms [42] and the panels above these (i.e. the tender front [87]). But the toolboxes of tank engines were painted and lined out as if they were tank sides [42].

The following components were painted black: smokebox with door and chimney, main frame and motion plate exteriors, splasher tops [88], tank tops, guard irons [88], cab roof exterior, footstep treads [42], brake gear [88], axles [88], axle ends [42], tyres, inside tender frames, tender interior [88], coal rails [42], hornplates, axleboxes, springs, buckles, hangers, lamps, lamp irons, toolboxes on tender tops [42], Ramsbottom safety valve.

The interiors of the main frames were tan [88, 93], (in the writer's opinion this must have looked very like "salmon"), and the cab interior walls were no doubt subject to a process of gradual darkening from their original grained finish. The cab roof interior is variously reported as green of an unspecified shade [88], and cream (which might well be dirty white [40]). The buffer beams and sockets were plain vermilion [88].

The lining was bold and striking. On the cab front and sides, (and on the cab rear of tank engines) tank, splasher and sandbox sides, and the sides and end of bunker and tender, was formed a border of colour B, separated from the general green colour by a triple stripe of white-black-white (fig. 5b, c) [59]. Boiler bands were black, edged with white, and a strip of brown, 3 in. wide [94], was painted on the boiler clothing each side [95]. This form of lining was introduced by Drummond in mid-1896, after he had used the Adams lining for a year [96, 97]. An interim form of lining is shown in the official photograph of F6 0-4-4T no. 366, turned out in July 1896 [98]. Here, although there is indeed a double white stripe, the corners of the panels are radiused (but with a sharper radius than Adams used). Drummond's lettering was at first L.S.W.R. (closed up and with stops [96, 97]), and still in the Adams size of $5\frac{1}{4}$ in. (n.b. [96]), but the legend was S W R (with or without stops [37]) from December 1895 to August 1897 [97, 99] and L S W from then until March 1898 [97]. Drummond's form of number plate appears [59] to have been a straight copy of the Caledonian Railway type [100], and fig. 3c has been drawn on this basis, since no specimen of a Drummond L S W R plate has come to light [101]. When the scheme had settled down, the dimensions of the lining came to be controlled by a number of factors which are set out below, but in general the white lines seem to have been one-eighth of an inch wide [102] and together with the black stripe made up a composite band not much more than 2 in. wide [59, 102] The outer brown margin could be up to $3\frac{1}{2}$ in. wide [59]. From 1895 to 1912 approximately the Company's arms were applied by transfer on the leading splasher of 4-4-0 engines. This badge was always of the same size — 17 in. total height (plate 1c [103]).

The widths of the lining appear to have been determined as follows [59]:

(i) Almost always, the widths were standardised for a given class of engine, and the widths were the same in all panels of one engine.

(ii) The composite stripe was usually the same width as the brown.

(iii) The brown band ran tangent to the top of the beading of the cab arch, or

(iv) The total width of the brown and the composite lines was small enough to lie between the square window frame of an Adams engine and the outer edges of the cab, or

(v) The widths were adjusted so that two brown stripes and one composite fitted the depth of the "neck" between the splashers, or

(vi) The widths were reduced so that the transfer of arms just fitted on the splasher without touching the lining, or

(vii) From about 1906 onwards, on new engines, the brown was standardised at 3 in. wide and the composite stripe at 2¼ in.

The Company initials were marked in gilt, shaded with black [75, 40], on the tender or tank sides, provided there was room. The angle of the shading seems to have varied a little, probably indicating that transfers were not used [59]. Generally, the letters were evenly spaced so as to divide the tender panel into five equal sections, but the vertical position was regularly such that the centre of the gilt portion of each letter was an inch above the half height of the painted panel (fig. 4c, d [59, 104]).

The engine number marked on the (Drummond) number plate appears to have been placed so that the tops of the figures were level with the initials on the tender [59]. When number plates were dispensed with in 1903, the transfer numerals which replaced them [72] were also aligned with the tender letters. Approximately until Drummond's death in 1912 the rule seems to have been, as before, top of numbers level with top of letters (fig. 4d [59]), but during and after the war the numbers sank a little so that the centre lines of the gilt parts of numbers and letters were level, or the lower edges of the gilt parts were level; the Urie engines were higher off the rail and the principle could not often be applied to them [59]. The marking of numbers on the buffer beams (front and rear [105]) followed the practice of Adams' time and examples are shown in figs. 5e, h, j, l [59]. 6 in. numbers came into use on the 4-6-0 classes from the start (fig. 5m [59]). The H15 class had some additions to the standard lining [59].

2.10 Passenger locomotives, October 1917 to December 1922.

Because of war conditions, Urie simplified the lining scheme in October 1917 [72]. That statement seems to be the only thing agreed about the livery of the period. There does not seem to be any specimen surviving of the locomotive colour, so two versions of the coach colour are listed with the other evidence below. It appears to me that the colour introduced by Urie in December 1914 (see Section 2.9) was a softer and rather darker green than that of Dummond. Probably the intention was to use the same colour on both locomotives and coaches but perhaps because of wartime conditions the engine colour later turned out lighter and yellower than the coach finish. The uncertainty about the LSWR green compounds the hilarious confusion about the inter-war SR greens.

Colours:

A: *Sage green* [72] Appendix 1.3
Light olive, no. 5-063 of BS 2660:1955
10 Y 5/6 [10] ★ 3
Dark grayish green, no. 5-061 of BS 2660:1955 10 GY 3/2 [40]
Grey green or olive green similiar to the shade used for a while by the Southern Railway (i.e. c. 1938 — colour A2 of Section 2.12) [40]
Green . . . took on a yellowish tinge [3, 5]
Yellowish green [107]
The green grew yellower to a lightish olive [83]
Olive green, quite light, like a ripe olive [108]
Rather brownish shade of green [109]
Sickly green [109]
The South Western has recently adopted an all-over pleasing shade of green, just a trifle darker than its engines. The company probably think the engines will gradually darken to match the coaches [110]
[The 1917 lining] made the green look a different shade, though, in fact, it was the same [94]
n.b., coach colours ★ 13 [111] and ★ 14 [112]

B: Gilt [113]
Yellow [113]

C: Vermilion [113]

D: Buff [113]

The boiler, firebox water-tube covers (if present), dome, Ramsbottom safety valve and casing, motion plate (if outside), wheel bosses, spokes and rims, cranks (if outside frames) and coal flare were all colour A.

Lining was applied to the following parts: cab front and sides (and splasher top if a continuation thereof), cab rear panel, splasher and sandbox sides, tank sides, bunker sides and end, valances, footsteps, tender sides and end, tender outside frames (exterior), panel on outside of Adams 4-4-2T toolbox, outside cylinders of Adams and Drummond engines. These were all edged with a black band, apparently with a standard width of 3 in., separated from the green paint by a thin white line. The cab sides of Adams locomotives so constructed continued to be lined out in two panels. Boiler bands were black and were edged in white. Urie's locomotives had a variation of lining on the cylinder clothing. A panel formed of a black edging with a white inside line was formed on the flank of the cylinder assembly. A photograph of G16 4-8-0T no. 494 shows that owing to the unusual depth and irregularity of the side tanks, the green panels there were cut short about 10 in. below the top edge. This engine conformed to the principle that top edge of letters=top edge of numbers, and had a pale ring of lining on the wheel bosses.

The colour of the frame interiors is not known for certain, but may have been colour D in conformity to the cab interiors.

As usual, many details of the engines were painted black, viz.: smokebox and door, forward-mounted Westinghouse pump, chimney, Ramsbottom safety valve, valve base and lever, brake gear, lamps, Westinghouse reservoir, cab roof, footstep treads, splasher tops, tank tops and ends, exterior of inside frames, ends of outside cylinders, guard irons, tyres, axle ends, tender top, tool box, coal box, coal space, coal rails, interior of tender frames, hornplates, axles, springs, spring buckles and hangers. Buffer beams and sockets were vermilion.

Bright parts comprised the edge of the smokebox front plate, and the handles and hinges of its door, the front edge of the guard irons, the buffer heads, handrails and outside motion (steel), cab spectacles end edging of splashers on Adams engines, Drummond safety valves, whistles and washout plugs (brass) and copper pipework. The list of bright parts was commonly not fulfilled, and officially such extra work as the polishing of the smokebox plate edges was not called for.

The lettering seems to have been applied in accordance with the same rules as before (Section 2.9), and the positioning of the cab-side numbers tended to be "lower edges of gilt parts level". The usual presentation on the front buffer beam was not, however, duplicated at the back, the engine number being written on the tender back as shown in fig. 5f [59], probably in yellow. But this may not have applied to tank engines, to judge from the markings of some engines after they had been taken over by the Southern Railway [59]. Power classification letters, A-K, were painted, usually in white but sometimes in yellow [114] on the valances behind the front buffer beams, but they were on the splashers of some Adams engines.

2.11 Southern Railway passenger locomotive liveries 1923-39.

The Southern locomotive livery was decided by July 1924 [115], but the shade of green employed as the basic colour has been a matter of controversy. In the period of office of R. E. L. Maunsell (1923-37) at least two distinguishable colours were used, of which the earlier seems to have been stock taken over from the L.S.W.R. But the available descriptions are excessively contradictory.

Colours:

A1: The L S W R sage green [116]
Described as "sage green", which, for anyone acquainted with a sage bush, it certainly was not. In fact the colour was a true olive green, exactly the colour of a good green olive [117], i.e. light olive 5Y 5/6.

The colour then in use by the L S W R ... olive green ... quite light [108]
No marked change from the final L S W R scheme [40, 118]
Cheese green [119]
Green contained too much yellow [72]
Yellowish green [107]
Light olive, no. 5-063 of BS 2660:1955 10 Y 5/6 [10] ★ 3
Moderate olive green, no. 5-065 of BS 2660:1955 5 GY 4/6 [76] ★ 14
Moderate olive green 7·5 GY 4/4 [76]

A2: *Dark green* [120] but hereafter referred to as Maunsell green
Olive green, prone to go blue Appendix 1.14
Presto green [121]
Sage green [72, 119]
Sage green to correspond with that used on coaches [108]
Sage or mid-green, not olive green [122]
The coach green, a deeper mid-green shade similar to the old Great Central Railway loco. colour [116], i.e.
Dark green 5 G 3/4 [123]
Dark apple-green — a good solid mid-green [117]
True olive green [124]
A more bluish green, mainly for new construction [40]
Locomotives just got darker [125]
Moderate olive green 2·5 GY 3/3 [126] ★ 5
n.b. this colour came from Ashford works and "Ashford repaints were never the same as Eastleigh" and "it (sample) is not dark enough" [127]. Appendix 3 tends to bear this out, but the colour is listed here under the identity it purports to have.
(Dark olive green 2·5 GY 2/4) [111] ★ 6
(Grayish olive green 5 GY 3/2) [128]
(Moderate olive green, Carter's no. 21, no. 221 of BS 381C:1964 5 GY 3/6 (near)) [48]
(Dark green 3 G 3/3 est.) [129]
(Dark grayish green 10 GY 3/2 approx.) [130]

B: Primrose, rather pale to start with, but richer later [131]
Strong orange 5 YR 7/11 [126] ★ 9
(Strong yellow 2·5 Y 7/10) [130]

C: Gilt [131]

D: *Stewarts red* [121]
(Vivid red, no. 537 of BS 381C:1964 7·5 R 4·5/16) [130]

E: Yellow ochre [121]

INSTRUCTIONS FOR PAINTING LOCOMOTIVES [121]

1. Scale and rust to be removed.
2. Primer — one coat lead, stopping as required.
3. For new locos., 6 coats filling.
For repairs, 4 coats filling.
4. Rub down.
5. One coat lead,
One coat Presto green for express locos., or one coat drop black for goods and shunting locos.
One coat varnish colour.
6. For new locos., 3 coats varnish.
For repairs, 2 coats varnish.

Smokebox —	1 coat drop black 1 coat Blundell-Speech Petrifying Paint.
Motion —	Red.
Buffer beam —	1 coat primer. 2 coats Stewarts red, 2 coats varnish.
Cab —	2 coats yellow ochre, 1 coat varnish.

Number and lettering — "as applied".

The livery (plate 3a) perpetuated the L S W R lining, and in some cases the engine number on the buffer beams was still in the small, plain figures used by the South Western (fig. 5n [58] shows the numbering of an engine in Southern livery). The tender described in section 2.10 showed that S R lettering was applied on top of the L S W R initials, and the two observations together suggest that there may have been very limited repainting of ex-L S W R engines after the grouping; merely the preparation of one panel on each side to receive the new legend and the number. The two incidents of engines with mixed L S W R and S R liveries in 1924-5, recorded by Bradley [132, 133] also point in this direction, unless "full South-Western livery" is intended to refer to the pre-1917 scheme. If some such economical practice was indeed the case, there would be a partial explanation of the different lining colours noted in the early S R period.

Lining. The layout of the lining was the same as the Urie L S W R pattern (fig. 5d) and the thin line was ¼ in. wide [120], the black edging [40, 72, 86, 107, 134] being nominally 3 in. wide [120]. The colour of the thin line was generally white [40, 72, 86, 107, 108, 130] but some newer engines had yellow lining out [40, 72 (implies), 134, 135], an idea which had already been in the files since Drummond's building of the F13 4-6-0s in 1905 [136]. However, the yellow lining was short-lived, white being substituted from 1925 onwards [72] or about 1930 according to two informants [40, 135]. But at the end of the period under discussion, there were several varieties of lining in use (see end of section).

Lettering. The style of the lettering was a striking extended type, which although probably influenced by American practice (see for instance the picture of a locomotive of the St. Clair Tunnel Co. [137]) actually conformed to the "Expanded Egyptian" type face invented in 1865 [138], which had passed into the pattern books of sign-writers around the turn of the century [139], when the Post Office indulged in it [140]. The standard form of the letters appears to have been that shown in fig. 6a [141], which agrees with an official drawing [142] and is confirmed by the measurements obtained from tender no. DS 3001 [104]. However, many if not all the class O2 0-4-4T engines had lettering approximately 9 in. longer than this (fig. 6b [58]), a curious discrepancy which may extend to other, less well photographed engines. There was some use of a distinctly smaller size as well [143]. These letters were painted on [131] in colour B [72, 131, 135] and no firm evidence of their being transfers has come to light. Gilt they never were, apparently [131, 135], in spite of the judicious wish-fulfilment practised by a reputable manufacturer of transfers for models [144].

Main numbering. The engine number, which until 1931 included a prefix letter indicating the home works (A-Ashford, B-Brighton, E-Eastleigh, W-Ryde), was painted below the company identification and the set of digits used (fig. 6d [58]) was subject to very slight variation in the form of the loops etc. The general size of these figures was 18 in. high [58, 104, 142, 143, 145], but variations to 16 in. (ex-L B S C R classes B4 and I3), 14 in. (class D1), 12 in. [142] (classes C14, F1, 0298 and no. 756) and in the other direction to 21 in. (class G16) have been noted [58]. A very few engines were tricked out with ex-L B S C R transfer numbers in gilt with black shading (fig. 6l [146]). This happened about 1935 [147] at Eastleigh, and no doubt started the rumour about gilt lettering in general. An example is shown in plate 3b. The works initial was ordinarily 3 in. high [148].

Number and name plates. With the large lettering went the use of oval number plates, which were fitted on the rear of tenders and bunkers, as well as in their characteristic position on the cab side panel of tender engines (no tank engine carried a cab side plate) [149]. Figs. 7d [64] and 7e [150] show examples of the type of plate used up to 1931; after that date, the works initial was ground off existing plates and a new design of plate, having the number in the centre with SOUTHERN above and RAILWAY below it, was fitted to new and renumbered engines [58]. The plates were of brass and the polished letters were at first set off by a black ground, as was the case with name plates also [131, 151], but some official drawings called for green [152] and in 1925 red was decided on [151,153]. The perpendicular edges of the plate were also red, and a narrow black band with the usual white (etc.) line was usually painted around the plate on the cab side to set it off [58]. Throughout the pre-war period, the style of S R name plates was constant, although they were of different shapes (figs. 8b, c [154], d [155]). Examples of makers' plates retained in S R days are shown in figs. 7b [154], c [64]. The name plate of no. 949 *Hecate* is included as a curiosity [155]

Subsidiary numbers. The engine number was also marked on the front and rear of engines in a variety of styles. A number of early S R photographs — and one of no. 187 taken as late as c. 1938 — shows buffer beams, both front and rear, with numbers still in the old L S W R style. While this may, as Mr. Tustin has suggested, have been the result of using up stocks of old transfers, it could well have been because minimum repainting was done after the grouping. The best support for this theory is a picture of O2 no. 189 in Southern lettering (with an E), no bunker plate, and

Table 1

	L S W type digits figs. 5n,s		SR serifed with 'Nº' figs. 5q,r		with 'E' fig. 5p		1938+ figs. 5t,u	
	off	near	off	near	off	near	off	near
4 in	527 614 628 643	35 42 55 71 117 unrebuilt 289 296 337 372 375 403 410 414 422 424 464 524 569 668 686 728 225 777 no 'Nº'					119 537	200 389 445 466 C1
5 in			119 286 709 1901	5 6 25 32 52 117 121 137 156 163 182 187 245 307 308 309 317 345 402 425 429 435 492 654 667 673 697 701 706 729 758 156 585 1315 no 'Nº'	639	174 310 681 699		
6 in		448 449 452 453 455 744 750 764 768 776 786 789 791 794 850 851 853 858 865		454 463 496 497 502 517 739 765 769 771 782 783 787 792 800 801 806 828 835 857 860 862 902 905 909 915 927 935		908 909 931	21C xxx	
8-9 in.								925 926 927 928 930 932 CC1

style n figures on the rear beam. Fig. 6n in fact shows a front buffer beam [58] and the results of an examination of front-end photographs undertaken by Mr. Tustin are set out in table 1. Whatever the reasons which led up to their use, the colour for styles n and s was probably gilt, not yellow.

After the irregularities of late 1923 [156], the standard style was that of fig. 5q [58], using figures in the style of figs. 6e [58] and 9d [146], the size generally appearing to be 5 in. high [58], but according to an Ashford drawing [157] in fact 4½ in. letters and 5 in. figures, on both front and rear beams. These figures were in colour C and black [131, 146] and might have been inherited by the S R from the S E C R [58]. Larger engines had 6 in. figures (of which fig. 9d happens to be a sample). The next stage was the incorporation on the beams of the works' initial — which may not have gone on for long, to judge by the paucity of pictures [156] — giving rise to style p [58]. And finally the 1931 renumbering solved the identification problem; the opportunity was taken to put the rear number (if there had in fact been one on the drag-beam) higher up in place of the rear number plate (fig. 5g [58] and plate 4a).

Before that, some minor varieties arose. 6 in. serifed figures with 'E' prefix were uncommon, but did exist, notably on "Schools" 4-4-0s. One case of the 5 in. legend E 639 all marked on the off side of the coupling has been noted, and at least four engines, nos. 119, 286, 709 and 1901, had the number so marked without any prefix at all [58].

In figs. 4 and 5, because of the necessity of using a small scale, the gold parts only of numbers and letters have been shown without any attempt to indicate shading. Because of this, complications may arise in locating figures for marking out. In fact this problem arose in the works also, and it was the practice to locate transfers by reference to the lower edge of the gold part; a horizontal line was printed on the backing paper of each transfer at this level to help the painter [146].

Having the number on the tender was handy for signalmen and loco-spotters, but if a tender had to be changed to keep an engine in service, it was not so good. There is a story that on one occasion a substitute tender had its figures altered by means of brown paper and paste. During the journey two numbers blew off one side and one from the other, so that the engine arrived at its destination with three apparent identities. It is not, however, suggested that this incident led to the livery changes of 1938. The following lists are of engines turned out of shops in the old (Maunsell) livery while the 1938 (Bulleid) livery was being settled [158]. It will be noted that three possibilities of lining existed within a short space of time.

Table 2

Early 1939: locomotives repainted in Maunsell 1931 livery with (presumed dark) green and yellow lining.

K10	4-4-0	345/94.
L11	4-4-0	173.
M7	0-4-4T	41/9.
T9	4-4-0	285.

Table 3

Mid 1939: locomotives repainted in Maunsell 1931 livery with black and yellow lining.

D15	4-4-0	469.
K10	4-4-0	136, 381.
L11	4-4-0	166, 407/39.
L12	4-4-0	416/31.
M7	0-4-4T	22, 33, 105/11/23, 356-7/75, 676.
O2	0-4-4T	197, 212.
T9	4-4-0	116, 311, 722.

Table 4

Late 1939: locomotives repainted in Maunsell 1931 livery with no lining.

A12	0-4-2	613/20/5/44.
D15	4-4-0	463.
E4	0-6-2T	2580.
H	0-4-4T	1158/269/79/310/523/40.
J	0-6-4T	1599.
L	4-4-0	1774.
L12	4-4-0	433.
N	2-6-0	1413/850.
R1	0-4-4T	1698.
S11	4-4-0	400.
T9	4-4-0	713-4/25.
U	2-6-0	1624-5, 1806-7/91, 1902.

The war naturally upset whatever plan had been made to standardise on one livery, and as a result of it a number of engines remained in a Maunsell livery right through the war. Table 5 lists engines which were still in this livery (or the goods version described in section 2.12) at the date of nationalisation, 1 Jan. 1948 [159]. These engines still had their S R number plates.

Table 5

1948: locomotives in existence in Maunsell livery.

(i) in service or in store.

A	0-6-0T	680S (not lettered).
A1/X	0-6-0T	2636/47*, 515S.
B1	4-4-0	1445/8/50/3.
B4	4-4-0	2051/68.
B4/X	4-4-0	2043.
D1	0-4-2T	2234/5/59/69/74/89/91, 2361.
E	4-4-0	1491.
E1	0-6-0T	2145.
E2	0-6-0T	2101
G6	0-6-0T	262.
H	0-4-4T	1324.
M7	0-4-4T	58.
P	0-6-0T	1325, 1555.
R	0-4-4T	1661.
R1	0-4-4T	1696/8.
R1	0-6-0T	1128
T	0-6-0T	500S (lettered S R).
0298	2-4-0WT	3329.
0395	0-6-0	3440.
Diesel		2.

*no. 2647 was withdrawn in Oct. 1951 and scrapped in 1955 in this livery.

(ii) withdrawn.

A1/X	0-6-0T	W 10, W 12.
A12	0-4-2	555. — ? see p. 23
D1	0-4-2T	2232/3, 2355.
T3	4-4-0	571.
X6	4-4-0	657/66.
0330	0-6-0	3334.

2.12 Goods locomotives, 1923-39.

These were painted black [72, 114, 160, 161] with dark green lining [72] — barely visible on photographs, but apparently in the same style as on passenger engines. Their lettering and numbers were subject to the same process of regularisation as the green engines' [160, 161] and eventually the lining was dispensed with from 1935-6 [160, 161]. A number of B4 class 0-4-0T engines were lined out in red in 1933-6 [162].

2.13 The new image, 1936-41.

It seems to have started with a complaint during the General Meeting of the Company in 1935. A shareholder felt that his railway was altogether too dowdy, and couldn't something be done to brighten up the appearance of the trains? He was told that a change *might* be considered [163], and nearly a year later, one of the electric trains was painted a vivid green [164]. After that there was a good deal of change on the locomotive side, difficult to define now because of the lack of good colour samples. First there was an extensive trial of paint of a new shade.

Colours:

A: *Dover green* [165]
  Olive green [156, 158, 166]
  Olive green, similar to the final LSWR colour [40]
  Tentatively to be identified with a coach colour:

  Moderate olive green 5 GY 4/3 [167]
  Dark yellowish green 10 GY 4/5 approx.) [168]
  A considerable quantity of stock has been painted in light green similar to that of the Highland Railway [169] (n.b. that green has been described as apple, sage and so on up the vegetable garden)

But after trials this was found not to come up to expectations [156]. "After some months service it turned khaki and often flaked badly" [170] and it was superseded by

B: Light green (later) known as malachite green [156]
  Bulleid green [170]
  Malachite green Appendix 1.15
  (Which) was accepted subject to being made one tone darker
  Pale emerald [135]
  Tentatively identified with colour no. 280 of BS 381C: 1964, i.e.
  Moderate green 5 G 5·5/6 [114]
  Dark yellowish green 2·5 G 4/6 [171]
  Dark green 5 G 3/4 to
  Strong green 5 G 4/6 est. [172]
  Dark green 7·5 G 3/6 [173, 174]
  Dark bluish green 10 G 3/5 [167]

  (Deep yellow green 7·5 GY 4/7 est.) [111] ★ 7
  (Dark green 4 G 3/4 est.) [175]
  (n.b., at present, B R coach green is
  Strong green 5 G 4/7
  discolouring to
  Dark yellowish green 2·5 G 3/3 [174])

C: Red [168] (assumed to be as D of section 2.11)

D: Yellow [156] (assumed as B of section 2.11)

E: Cream [156] (assumed to be a variety of yellow — cf B in section 2.11)

F: Dark green [156] (assumed to be Maunsell green)

With the new greens went a new form of lettering, which in these pages will be called Bulleid lettering. The letters were adapted from the type face which had been used in advertising and other print for some years (see section 6.9). The standard form for locomotives was as shown in fig. 6h [176] and a component letter in fig. 9c [176]. The letters were gilt with an internal black line [165]. With these letters a new style of numeral was used; this was gilt with plain black shading (fig. 9g [146]), which served both for cab side and buffer beam (fig. 5u [58]), and presumably also for the rear panel of the tender, although evidence is lacking. Besides the 9 in. size, there were letters and figures 6 in. high for use on smaller engines (fig. 9h shows three gilt letters as they were spaced out on the transfer backing sheet [146]). The proportions of the two sizes of letter were slightly different, as the black and gilt edgings were of a constant ¼ in. width. Fig. 6g shows a slightly differing form of the inscription; it is sketched from a very small photograph of 0-4-4T no. 1706 [177].

The experimental asymmetric numbering of one engine in 1938 — one number was on the smoke deflector instead of on the cab side [166] was not adopted; ordinary symmetrical marking was the rule for engines and the Bulleid lettering was brought into use from mid-1938 onward [158], although there was an overlap period during which both Maunsell and Bulleid lettering was being applied. The first Eastleigh engine having been given Bulleid lettering in June 1938 [166], the first Ashford example was as late as November 1939. Still further to confuse the situation, all known varieties of lining were being applied concurrently. Tables 6 to 10 below list all the available notes [158] on repaintings in Bulleid livery during the transition from peace to war; after March 1941 (Eastleigh) and July 1941 (Ashford) all engines repainted were coloured black, except for classes LN, N15 and V [158]. The lining colours are denoted in these tables by pairs of code letters, the legend being: **B**=black, **G**=dark green, **W**=white, **Y**=yellow. The lining patterns seem to have been the same as under Maunsell, i.e. fig. 5d with the lighter colour as the lining and the darker as the picking out [58], although the amount of black paint on the side view of the engine was reduced by painting the smoke deflectors and the coal flare green and lining them out. Lining was dispensed with from September 1939 [158], except for classes LN, N15 and V, which retained it until they were painted black after April 1942 [156, 178].

Table 6

1938-40: locomotives repainted with Bulleid lettering on green A.

H1	4-4-2	**BY**: 2037.
H2	4-4-2	**GY**: 2423-4/6.
H15	4-6-0	**GY**: 332, 491.
		BY: 477/82/5/8.
LN	4-6-0	**GY**: 852/5-6/8-9/61-3.
N15	4-6-0	Trials engine: 749, see [166].
		GY: 448/52/5, 745/75/90.
		BY: 450/3-4/6-7, 736/40-2/4/7/

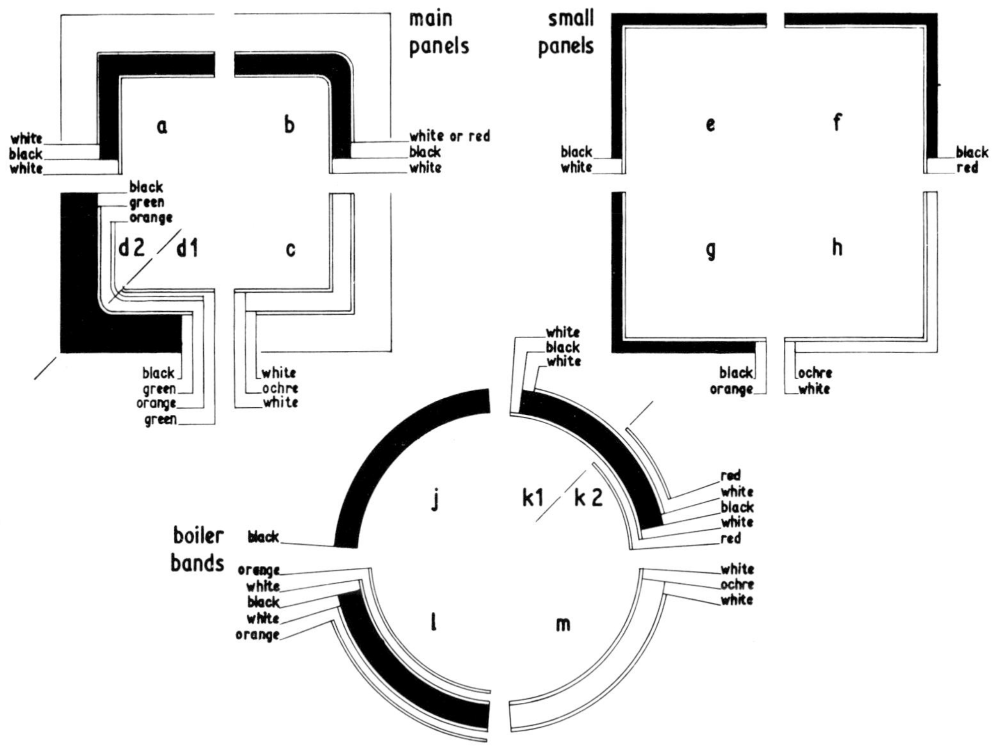

Fig. 1 LSWR locomotive lining before 1883 not to scale

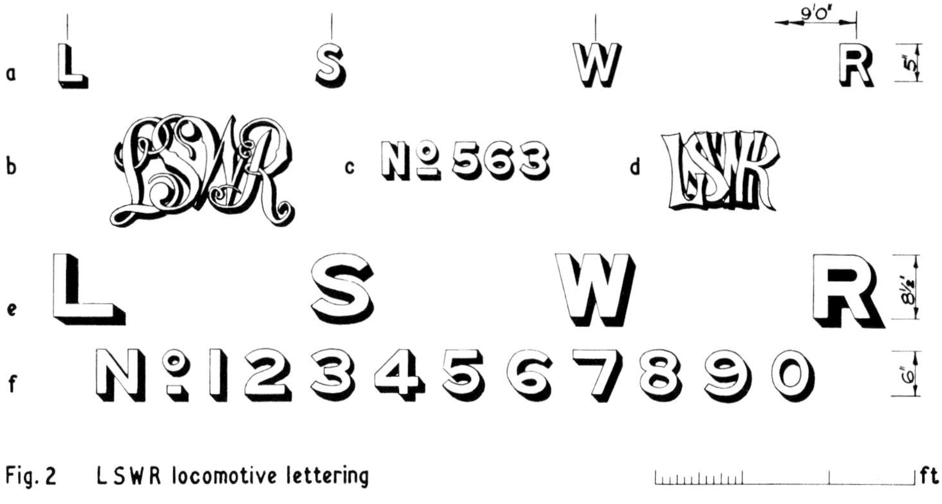

Fig. 2 LSWR locomotive lettering

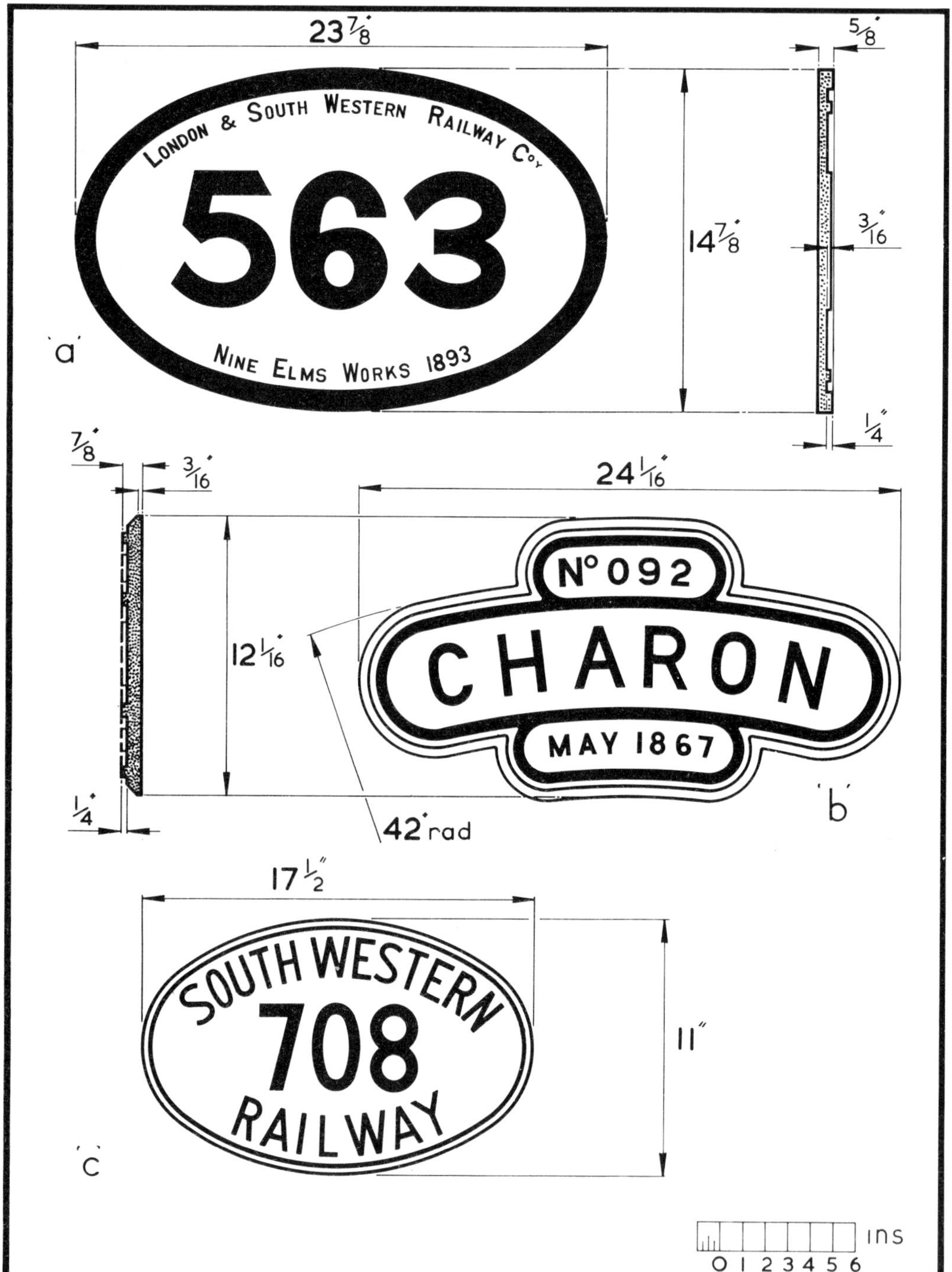

Fig. 3 LSWR locomotive number plates

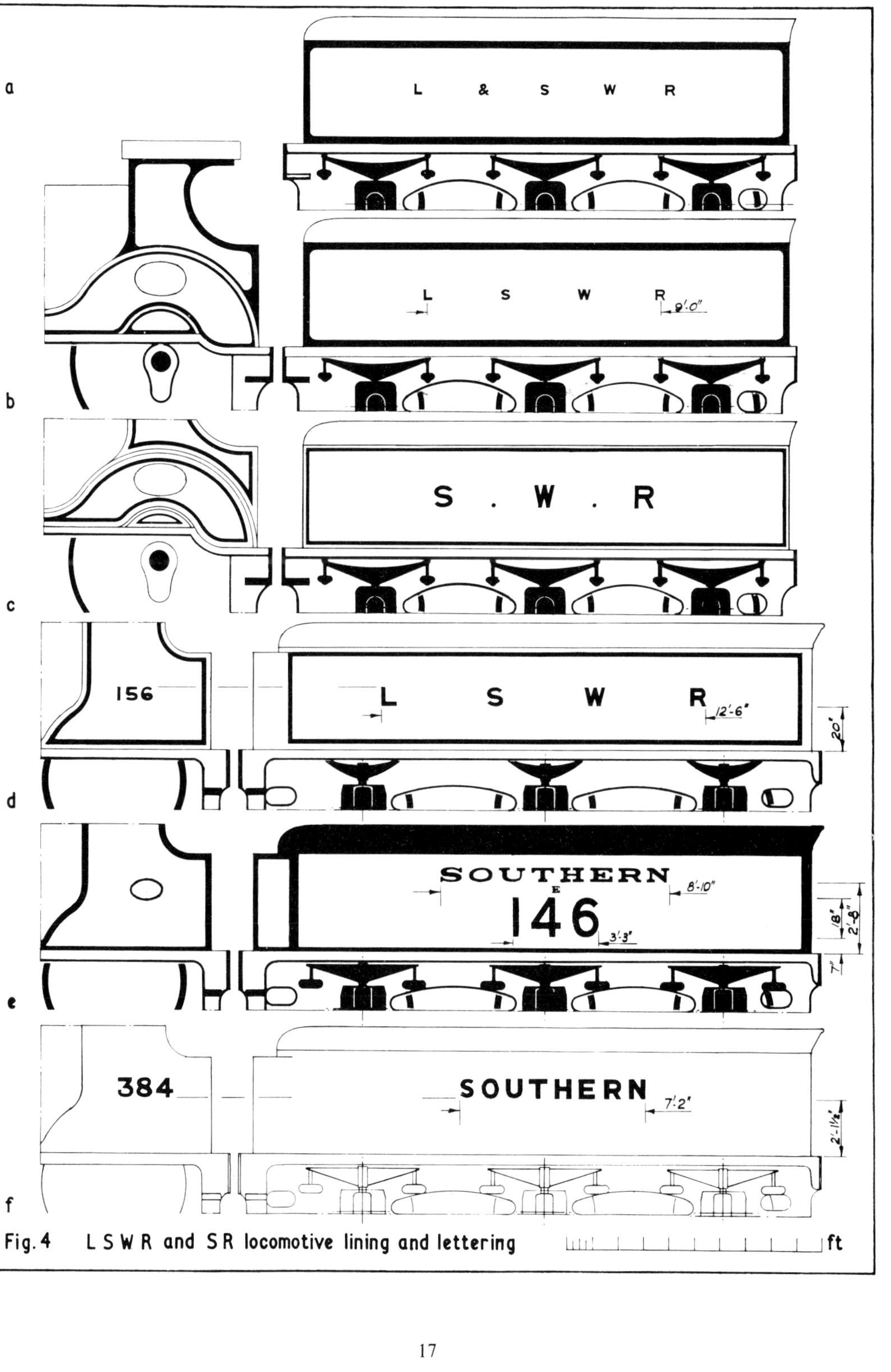

Fig. 4 L S W R and S R locomotive lining and lettering

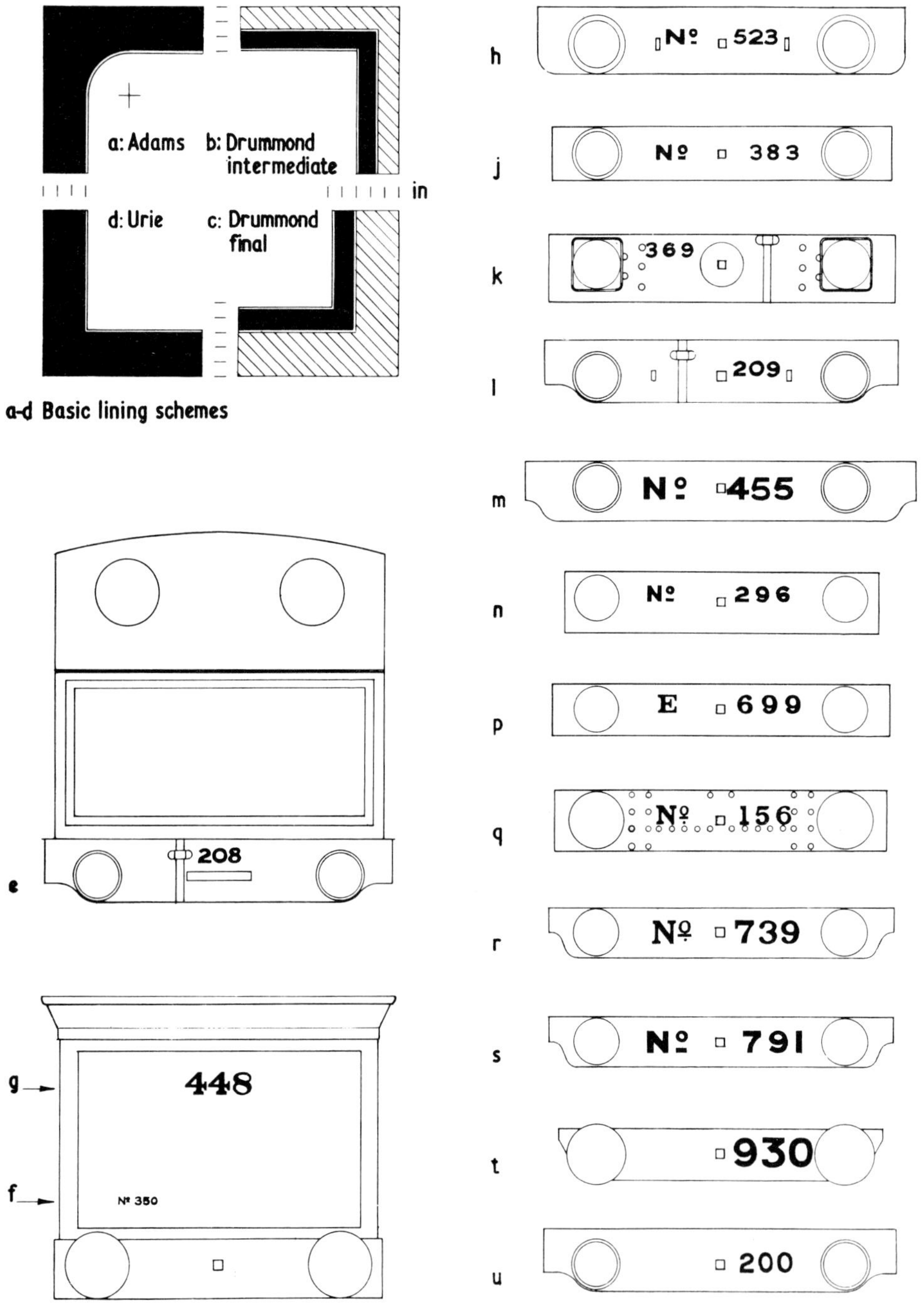

Fig. 5 Locomotive lining and end numbering

Fig. 6 S R locomotive lettering

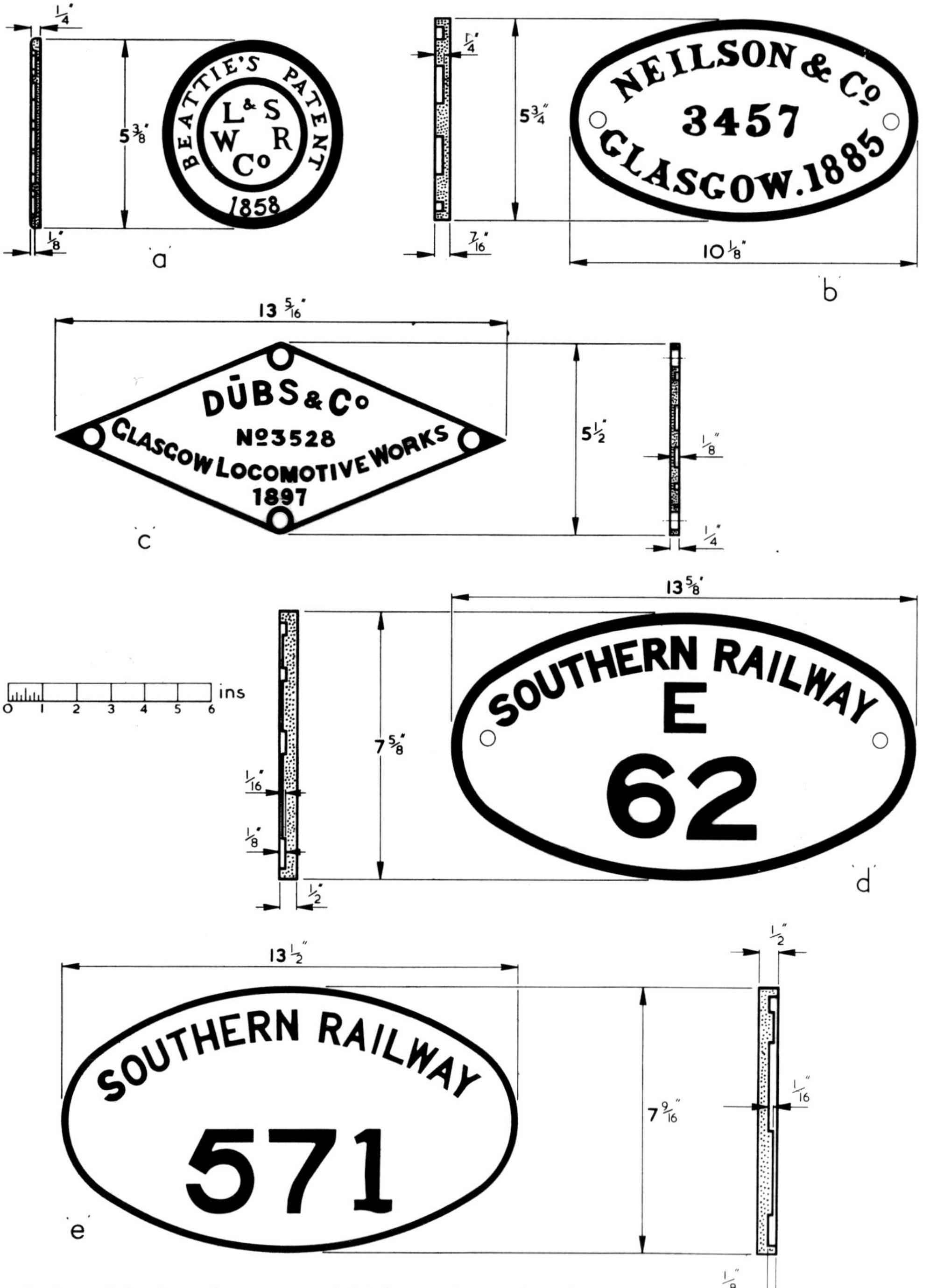

Fig. 7 LSWR works plates and SR locomotive number plates

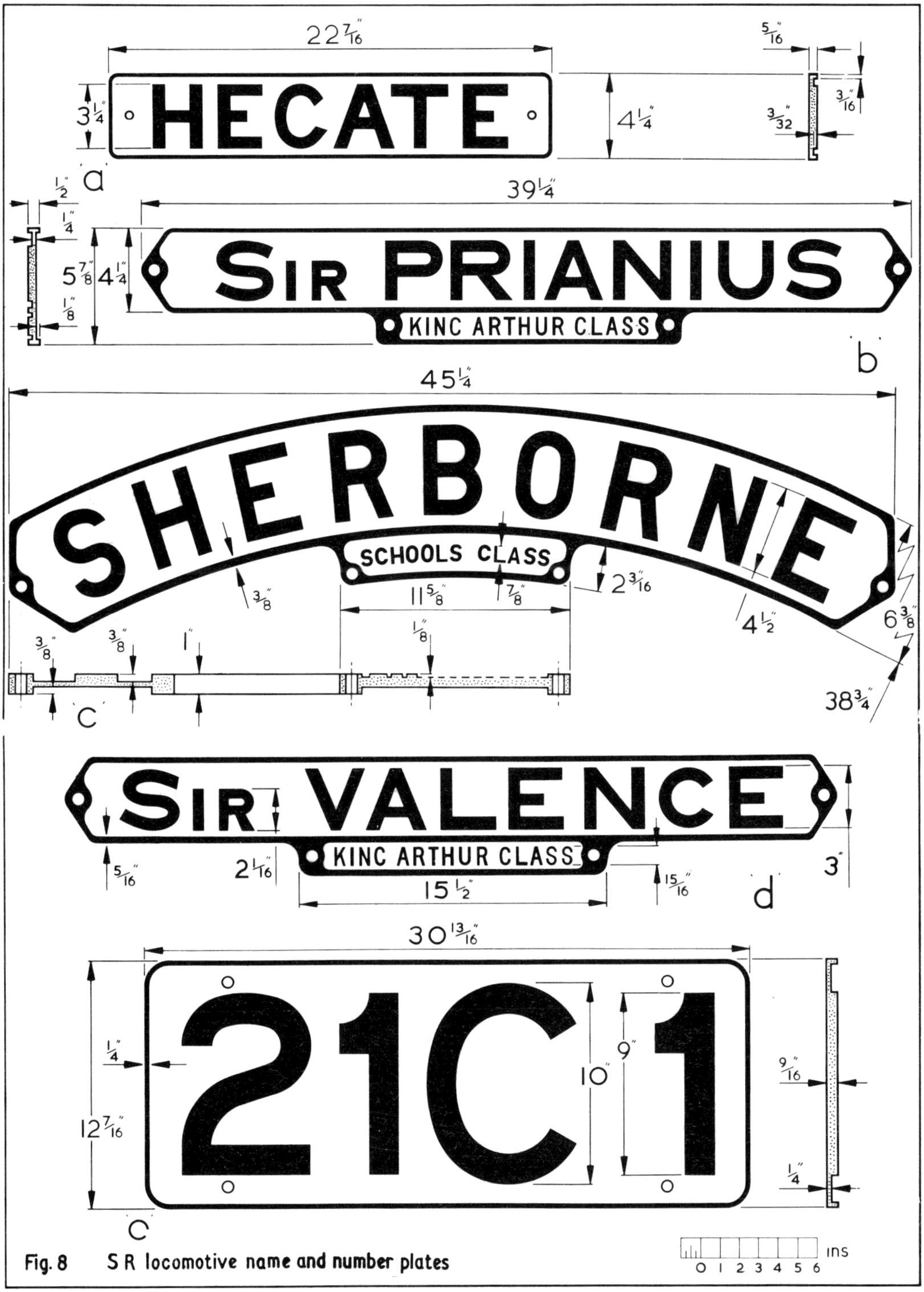

Fig. 8 S R locomotive name and number plates

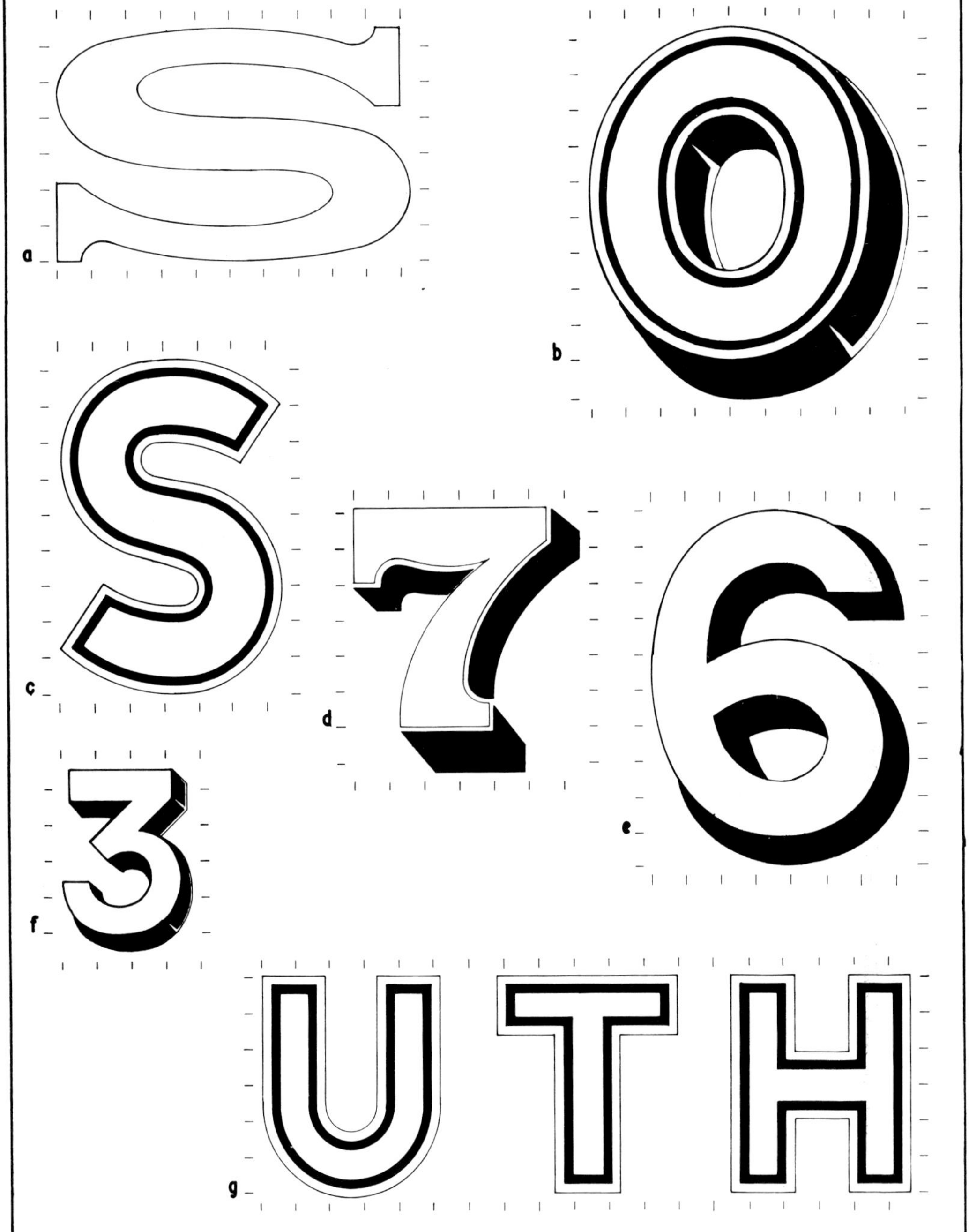

Fig. 9 Examples of S R locomotive lettering

		53/5/68/70/2-4/7/80-1/6/8/ 93/5/9, 800/3/5-6.
N15/X	4-6-0	**BW**: 2327/9-30/2.
T9	4-4-0	**BW**: 119.
V	4-4-0	**BW**: 937.
		GY: 912/29.
		BY: 900/2/11/7-8/20/7.

Table 7

Late 1938 to early 1941: locomotives repainted with Bulleid lettering on green B.

LN	4-6-0	**GY**: 851/62-3.
		BW: 853.
		BY: 850/4/6-65.
N15	4-6-0	**BW**: 746/66/89.
		BY: 448/52/5-7, 739/43-5/8/50-1 /4/63/5/7/9/75-6/9/81-5/7, 790-2/4/6-8, 802/4-5.
N15/X	4-6-0	**BY**: 2328/31/3.
V	4-4-0	**GY**: 919/35.
		BW: 906/21/5-30/2.
		BY: 901/4-5/7/9-10/3/5-6/9/22/ 4/6/8-34/6-7.

Table 8

Late 1939: locomotives repainted with Bulleid lettering on Maunsell green.

B4/X	4-4-0	**BY**: 2044.
H1	4-4-2	**BW**: 2038-40.
H15	4-6-0	**BW**: 330, 473/5/86, 524.
I1/X	4-4-2T	**BY**: 2007, 2597.
LN	4-6-0	**BW**: 864.
L11	4-4-0	**BY**: 174.
N15	4-6-0	**BW**: 449/51, 736-8/43/8/51-2/4/ 64/76/82/4-5/7, 802.
N15/X	4-6-0	**BW**: 2333.
S15	4-6-0	**BY**: 846.
V	4-4-0	**BW**: 908/14/23-4/33-4/8.

Table 9

Late 1939 to 1941: locomotives repainted with Bulleid lettering on Maunsell green, unlined.

A1/X	0-6-0T	2655.
A12	0-4-2	555/97, 606/12/4/24/9/36/43/9.
B1	4-4-0	1446.
B4	4-4-0	2063/70/4.
D1	4-4-0	1246, 1477.
D1	0-4-2T	2229/39-40/52-3/5/84, 2358, 2699.
D3	0-4-4T	2384.
D15	4-4-0	464/7-8/72.
E1/R	0-6-2T	2124, 2608/95.
E4	0-6-2T	2497, 2562/7/81.
E5	0-6-2T	2399.
F1	4-4-0	1140/95.
H	0-4-4T	1264/76, 1305/9/22, 1550/1.
H2	4-4-2	2421-2/5.
H15	4-6-0	478/83/7/90. see [178].
H16	4-6-2T	519.
I1/X	4-4-2T	2001/3/6/10, 2595/9, 2602.
I3	4-4-2T	2021/8/75/83/8/90.
J	0-6-4T	1596.
K	2-6-0	2339/46/8/51/3.
K10	4-4-0	137-8/40-1/3, 343/86/8/91.
L	4-4-0	1768/70-1.
L1	4-4-0	1757.
L11	4-4-0	148/57-8/61/4-5/71/5, 406/8-10/ 35-7/40-1.
L12	4-4-0	415/9-20/3/30/4.
M7	0-4-4T	22/7, 44, 50-1/3/7, 106-7/24-5/8/ 31/3, 249/53/6, 324/74/6-8/80, 667-9/71/3/5.
N	2-6-0	1403, 1821/5/47/78.
O2	0-4-4T	179/83/93/8, 201/23-5/9-31.
R	0-4-4T	1661.
S11	4-4-0	398, 402.
S15	4-6-0	497-8, 502/5-7/11-3, 824/6/9-30/ 8-9/41-2,
T1	0-4-4T	1, 2, 4, 7-8, 10/5-7, 358-60/4/6-7.
T3	4-4-0	563.
T9	4-4-0	113-4/7/20-2, 284/7, 305/7/36, 702-3/7-9/11/7-8/23/8/30-1.
T14	4-6-0	444/7.
U	2-6-0	1610/5-7/9/22-3/6/37-8, 1791/4, 1805/92/8, 1904.
X2	4-4-0	586.
X6	4-4-0	658-9.
0415	4-4-2T	3520.

Table 10

Late 1940 to early 1941: locomotives repainted with Bulleid lettering on green B, unlined.

A12	0-4-2	600/38.
D1	0-4-2T	2605/27.
D15	4-4-0	466/70-1.
E1/R	0-6-2T	2094-5, 2610.
H15	4-6-0	334-5, 474/6/89.
H16	4-6-2T	516.
I1/X	4-4-2T	2004, 2596, 2600.
I3	4-4-2T	2081.
K	2-6-0	2337/50.
K10	4-4-0	389.
L11	4-4-0	158/69-70.
L12	4-4-0	429.
M7	0-4-4T	54/6, 104/27, 242.
N15	4-6-0	738.
O2	0-4-4T	200.
S15	4-6-0	500/8, 825/7/31/3.
T9	4-4-0	115, 302/10, 704/16/22.
T14	4-6-0	459.

2.14 The black years, and on to nationalisation, 1941-8.

After mid-1941, as noted previously, all repainting was done in black, and in an effort to brighten up the drabness, the SR introduced a variation on the Bulleid lettering. Probably the first purchase of transfers had run out, and it was no great task to design a new style. A second ostensible reason was to reduce the amount of gold leaf used [179]. The new transfers, later known as "sunshine" lettering, were of the pattern shown in plate 4a, figs. 6j [180, 181] and 9b [146]; they were intended to be of two colour combinations, viz:

(i) yellow ("old gold") [179] with black interior line and green blocking, with highlights in yellow [156, 182, 183].

(ii) gilt with black interior line and blocking, with highlights in gilt [179], for the "150 remaining green engines", some of which were probably already black at that time [184]. It seems questionable whether transfers of this colouring were in fact used during the war [182, 183] or at all [183, 185, 186].

Type (i) was used all through the latter years of the war; Mr. Bradley noted unshaded letters on black engines toward the end of the war [156]; this might indicate the use of left-over Bulleid style transfers, or perhaps the surplus gilt and black type (ii) if it existed.

Numbers in yellow-with-green were designed to match the letters, and reduced-size numerals in yellow and black [182] in the style of figs. 6k [58, 181] and 9f [146]; in theory there would have been numbers in gilt and black as well, for green engines, but no information seems to be recorded on this topic. Tender end numbers were still being applied at nationalisation — in fact until at least July 1948 [186] — with the curious distinction that Brighton put them on all colours of engines, and Eastleigh only on green ones [185].

The size of the buffer beam numbers was nominally 6 in. high [181, 182], but intended to be reduced to 4½ in. [182] (fig. 9f [146]) on the following classes of engine, which were also to have 6 in. transfers on the tanks and bunker [182]: A1/X[2]; B4 (0-4-0T)[1,2]; C14[2]; 02[2,4]; P[2]; T[1,2]; 756; 757[5]; 1302[2]; 0298; 0415[2]; 0458[1]; Diesel[2]; (also R1 (0-6-0T)[1,2]; USA[2]. [149]). Legend [149]: 1=Bulleid lettering, 2="Sunshine" lettering, 3=some had 9 in. side transfers, 4=9 in. side transfers for Isle of Wight engines, 5=probably did not ever carry this style.

Malachite green commenced to be used again in spring 1946, and in addition to the express engines, classes LN, MN, N15, V and WC/BB, was applied to a small number of secondary engines. The lining was regularly black and yellow.

Table 11

1946-8: locomotives (other than express passenger) repainted in malachite green S R livery.

H1	4-4-2	2037-41 (but 2039 ended its life with a black boiler).
H2	4-4-2	2421-6.
J	4-6-2T	2325-6.
L	4-4-0	1761/4/6-70/2-5/7-81.
L1	4-4-0	1754-9/83-9.
M7	0-4-4T	242/3 (unlined), 676.
N	2-6-0	1817/54.
T9	4-4-0	119 (lined black and white).

On the Isle of Wight, the O2s, A1/X no. W 13 and E1 nos. W 1/4 were painted malachite green.

2.15 Bulleid liveries for Bulleid engines [159].

Presumably stemming from the livery developed by the L M S in 1937 for the "Coronation Scot", Bulleid developed a bold livery in horizontal stripes of green and yellow. The mock-up fitted to no. 935 *Sevenoaks* in February 1938 (there were three versions, with three, four and five yellow stripes respectively [59, 187, 188]), decorated with the standard 1931 number plates and straight name plates, in addition to the bold company identification and number and a "sun's face" plate on the smokebox door [149], seems intended to show just how bad streamlining could look, yet many of the principles involved were transferred to *Channel Packet* with visible success.

As first turned out, no. 21 C 1 had the whole side area painted malachite green, relieved by three stripes of yellow. The paint had a matt finish, and although it has been said not to require varnishing [156], it was the practice at Eastleigh later on to apply one or two coats [189] (is the difference between matt and gloss finish the explanation of the apparent difference [186] between pre-war and post-war malachite greens? See section 2.13). The upper stripe on no. 21 C 1 ran touching the level of the cut-down part at the rear of the tender, forward along the engine casing. The middle stripe had as its bottom edge the lowest part of the window frame. The bottom stripe was placed as far above the valance as the top stripe was below the rainstrip. Within the lower pair of bands so formed, the name, number and Company plates were mounted symmetrically with respect to the driving axle, the cab windows and the length of the tender panel. These six plates were centred half-way between the yellow bands. The number plates, of which there were three on each engine, one above the buffer beam and the others on the cab sides, were 2 ft. 10¾ in. x 12½ in. [190]. The plates marked SOUTHERN were 7 ft. 0 in. x 10¾ in., with 9⅛ in. letters [190]; both types were cast in gunmetal and all except the inscriptions was painted red [58]. The name plates were *brass*, 6 ft. 1¼ in. long and 2 ft. 6¼ in. dia. of circle. The central roundel was an enamelled plate, 16¾ in. dia. [191]. As first painted, the livery looked uneven because the upper pair of stripes appeared somewhat cramped together, and so the middle stripe was lowered by an amount equal to its own width. The plates were left where they were and in fact the middle stripe was only a little higher than a tangent to the name plate. From no. 21 C 3 onwards, the "Merchant Navies" only had name plates and the annular (for a short while horse shoe-shaped) plate on the smokebox door, which had also been a characteristic feature of the first two engines.

Of the later eight, most were in a plain black livery [58, 159], relieved only by red buffer beams and yellow and green transfers [183]. The size of transfer used was 9 in. on the cab sides, although nos. 21 C 3/4 had letters C with a black interior line, 10 in. high, and nos. 21 C 5-10 had the same size without the interior line. Nos. 21 C 11-30 had 9 in. Cs *without* a line. The tender side lettering was a normal 9 in. presentation in the colours appropriate to the livery (see section 2.14). The front end numbers carried above the buffer beam were also variable, and confusingly so on 21 C 3, which was photographed in grey paintwork with a 9 in. number and almost immediately finished off in green with 6 in. front numbers. In the cases of nos. 21 C 3-5 the C was larger than the figures, but this feature seems finally to have been eliminated after July 1942; plain 6 in. figures and C without the in-line became the rule. From April 1942, all repainting was in black.

The livery of the "West Country" light Pacifics was not subject to anything like the same variation. Nos. 21 C 101-70 were turned out in green with three yellow stripes in approximately the same places as on the "MN"s (plate 3c). All parts below the level of the valance edge were black, except for the buffer beams, although Eastleigh often repainted the wheels green, as on the larger Pacifics. The rear panel of the tender was also green. The name plates were gunmetal, 8⅛ in. deep, the class name plates 2 ft. 7⅛ in. long, and the shields 20 in. x 23¾ in. over projections [192].

The Q1 0-6-0 engines appear to have been painted black, relieved only by red buffer beams and appropriate transfers (without in-line), throughout their existence.

The electric locomotive, no. CC 1, was finished in a livery which may have been the "photographic" version of that used on the Pacifics. It was grey with three horizontal white stripes about an inch wide. The two lower bands passed through the ventilating grilles along the sides and swept down to a point above the buffer beams in true "Coronation Scot" fashion. The upper stripe formed a separate focus and came to a point above the route indicator board. The engine number was only marked on the buffer beams; it just fitted either side of the coupling and was in standard 9 in. transfers [159]. In about November 1944 the engine was repainted in malachite green. The number was again on the red buffer beams and the word SOUTHERN was marked in large gilt (*sic*) letters on the sides, together with three yellow stripes which did not now extend on to the end face of the body [193]. No. CC 2, built in 1945, was painted similarly. A later addition, made at Brighton in 1947, was a board with a duplicated SOUTHERN and a bisecting electric flash above each end. The lettering was only about 3 in. high, and presumably in yellow and black.

2.16 A postscript.

The liveries of S R engines under British Railways' ownership find no place in this book. That task remains for a future writer in this series. But a glance this side of 1947 is in order. It may be said that it took BR twenty years to shake off the effects of the war in respect of livery development. The attempt which was made in 1938 to integrate the style of locomotives, carriages and buildings can now be seen to have been a harbinger of recent BR changes. A specific example of the process is the design of the number plates on the early Bulleid Pacific engines. In these, the letters and numbers were of a face which can be seen to have anticipated the Kinnear alphabet adopted by BR as used for example on the D 1000 class engines [194]. The Bulleid plates were no mere imitation of a preceding style, such as the G W R adhered to, but an interpretation of what had gone before in the light of current ideas on lettering. These plates represent a progression from the Gill Sans script used before the war, but because of the war there was no development from them. Instead, there was the wartime expedient of putting the "sunshine" back into the lettering — a justifiable, but retrograde, complication of the Bulleid letter face, which, perhaps because the latter was itself an elaboration of a basic alphabet, produced a mess. The "blocking" of a letter adds to its impression of solidity (reliability in the "image"), whereas Gill's alphabet relies for strength on its clarity and proportion.

Taking a still longer view, the livery changes made by the L S W R over the years represented a move away from the use of traditional schemes and plain lettering carried out with a palette of landscape colours, through a phase of reliance on overseas ideas and, under the S R into a period when there was a drive to achieve perfection of form with little regard for function (an example of which was the fashion for arranging continuous bands of colour along the whole length of a train). The reconciliation of the traditional, the functional and the fashionable was what the 1938 livery changes were about, but the experiment was terminated by the war. By 1948 the atmosphere was not conducive to experiments, the overriding want being one for the familiar and understood, moderated by a recognition of functional needs. How else can one explain the slightly incongruous combination of the traditionally-derived BR liveries with the Gill alphabet invented a generation later than the main colour schemes?

References

1. Bradley, D. L., *Locomotives of the London and South-Western Railway,* Solihull, Railway Correspondence and Travel Society, pt. 1, 1965, p. 13. (n.b., pt. 2 pub. Lichfield, Staffs., 1967).
2. Unidentified engraving, Mr. N. Pattenden's collection.
3. *Railway Magazine,* v. 80, pp. 141-2 (Feb. 1937).
4. Battley, H. H., coloured sketches and contemporary paintings used by E. W. Twining as a basis for an illustration in Bennett, A. R., *Historic Locomotives.*
5. Ellis, C. H., *The Trains we Loved,* London, George Allen and Unwin, 1955, p. 181.
6. Ellis, C. H., *The South Western Railway,* London, George Allen and Unwin, 1956, p. 36.
7. Ellis, *SWR,* p. 70.
8. Ellis, C. H., *Some Classic Locomotives,* London, George Allen and Unwin, 1949, p. 44.
9. Matched from patent plate in the Museum of British Transport, Apr. 1968 (see fig. 7a) — but it is not at all certain that the colour or for that matter the plate is associated with a locomotive.
10. Kerley, G. K. J., Nichols, K.O'B. and Howard Turner, J. T., private communication of considered opinion.
11. Marshall, C. F. D., (revised by R. W. Kidner), *History of the Southern Railway,* London, Ian Allan, 1963, v. 1, p. 171.
12. Burtt, F., *L S W R Locomotives, a Survey 1872-1923,* London, Ian Allan, n.d. but c. 1950, p. 10.
13. Bradley, op. cit. 1, p. 14.

14. Twining, E. W., private communication to Mr. L. Ward.
15. *Locomotive Magazine*, v. 18, fp. 247 (Dec. 1912). See also Ellis, C. H., *The Pictorial Encyclopaedia of Railways*, Feltham, Paul Hamlyn, 1968, colour plate f.p. 112.
16. Ellis, *SWR*, p. 81.
17. Ahrons, E. L., (ed. L. L. Asher) *Locomotive and Train Working in the Latter Part of the Nineteenth Century*, Cambridge, Heffer and Sons, 1953, v. 5, p. 90 (reprinted from the *Railway Magazine* of 1920-1).
18. Ellis, *SWR*, p. 96.
19. Kerley, G. K. J., from examination of photographs.
20. Ellis, *SWR*, p. 78.
21. Ellis, C. H., private communication.
22. Carter, E. F., *Britain's Railway Liveries . . . 1825-1948*, London, Harold Starke, 1963, p. 128.
23. Bradley, op. cit., 1, p. 15.
24. Ellis, *SWR*, p. 120.
25. BTHR LSW 5/3: L S W R, *Tender for ten four-wheels coupled bogie tank engines for passenger trains, 1884* (dated June 1884).
26. Bushell, A. M., in *Railway Magazine*, v. 63, p. 408 (Nov. 1928).
27. *Locomotive Magazine*, v. 39, p. 305 (14th Oct. 1933).
28. Thompson, W. B., in *Railway Magazine*, v. 63, p. 408 (Nov. 1928).
29. Burtt, op. cit., p. 25.
30. Walker, J. B., in *Railway Magazine*, v. 63, p. 320 (Oct. 1928).
31. Ellis, *SWR*, p. 95.
32. L S W R, unidentified water-colour drawing, believed to date at least from c. 1910, of 4-4-0 no. 144 (1881), in a livery which approximates to that described in section 2.5, but with lining based on the use of broad green bands, with a broad black outer band and a thin orange line standing clear of the green, inside. The boiler bands are also shown as plain green with a separate thin orange line. The drawing has been in the possession of Mr. L. Ward's family for over a generation.
33. Bradley, op. cit., 1, fig. 71.
34. Russell, G. A., private communication of details of model of 4-4-0 no. 471 (1884) exhibited in Inverness Museum. The model was built by Mr. E. W. Porter, Resident Engineer of the Caledonian Canal, in the years 1890-4. The livery is fairly close to that described in section 2.7, but the white lining is separated from the black picking out by a thin green line, and the footplate angle has simply a white edging. The wheels are green with black tyres and axle ends; the latter have white lining. The wheel bosses have a plain white line and the covers on the running plate above the slide bars are green with a white edge. The reversing shaft and all inside faces of the frames (including parts in front of the smokebox) are red. The cab interior is reddish brown no. 1-018. The numbers and lettering are gilt, with black shading on the buffer beams, and *red* shading, highlighted with white, on the tender sides, where the inscription LSWR has a gap as though an ampersand has been left out.
35. Hambleton, F. C., "Locomotives Worth Modelling", in *Model Engineer* v. 93, pp. 202-5, (30th Aug. 1945).
36. Ellis, *SWR*, p. 135.
37. Bradley, op. cit., 1, p. 16.
38. Hewitt, L. B., in *Railway Magazine*, v. 63, p.320 (Oct. 1928), referring to Beattie engines at c. 1898.
39. Maskelyne, J. N., in *Model Railway News*, v. 29, p. 188 (Sept. 1953).
40. Knight, D. W., private communication of colours identified by his relatives' recollection.
41. L S W R, unidentified drawing, generally similar in style to ref. 32 and also believed to date from at least c. 1910, showing 4-4-0 no. 461 (1884). Livery dark green overall, black picking out and white lining — not very clearly done.
42. Nichols, K. O'B., from examination of photographs.
43. BTHR LSW 1/186, minute no. 208.
44. Hewitt, H. D., and Shapcote, H., in *Railway Magazine*, v. 63, p. 320 (Oct. 1928).
45. BTHR LSW 1/186, minute no. 296.
46. Hambleton, F. C., "Locomotives Worth Modelling" in *Model Engineer*, v. 93, p. 135 (9th Aug. 1945).
47. Matched from model by the brothers Coates, in the Science Museum, South Kensington (exhibit no. 1896/81).
48. Carter, op. cit., colour chart.
49. This was the colour chosen in 1961 for the second restoration of locomotive no. 563 at the Museum of British Transport, Clapham. Allowance was made for discolouration of the Coates brothers' model (ref. 47) which was used as a guide. (Information made available by Mr. J. Scholes).
50. Matched to no. 563 in 1964.
51. Colour photograph reproduced in Simmons, T. M., *Railways to the End of the Nineteenth Century*, London, HMSO, 1964, pl. 20.
52. Pettigrew, W. F., *A Manual of Locomotive Engineering*, London, Charles Griffin, 3rd edn. revised 1909, pp. 343, 346.

53. L S W R, *Specification of 0-4-2 Mixed Traffic Locomotive*, 1886.
54. L S W R, unnumbered side-view drawing, *New 7 ft. 1 in. Express Engine and Tender,* dated 14th March 1893.
55. Hambleton, F. C., private communication of dimensions and details established for the restoration of no. 563, from drawing cited in ref. 54 and other sources.
56. Note the series of cracked axles experienced in W. G. Beattie's time — see Bradley, op. cit., 1, pp. 63, 117.
57. Burtt, op. cit., p. 43.
58. Drawn from photographs.
59. From examination of photographs.
60. Burtt, op. cit., p. 49.
61. Drawn from the replica plate attached to no. 563 in 1948.
62. Cf. Watling, J., drawing of G E R plate of 1882 in *HMRS Journal,* v. 4, p. 29 (1962).
63. Burtt, op. cit., p. 11.
64. Drawn from a plate in the Museum of British Transport, Clapham.
65. BTHR LSW 1/186, minute no. 572.
66. *The Rambler* (contemporary periodical), quoted by J. N. Maskelyne in *Model Railway News,* v. 34, p. 244 (Oct. 1958).
67. Burtt, op. cit., p. 8.
68. Pemble, —, in *Model Railway News,* location not known.
69. Hambleton, F. C., "Locomotives Worth Modelling", in *Model Engineer,* v. 99, pp. 474-6 (4th Nov. 1948).
70. Anon., *HMRS Livery Register no. 1, Caledonian Railway Locomotives, 1883-1923,* London, HMRS, n.d. but 1965, passim.
71. Casserley, H. C., dated photographs of nos. 59, 60, 109 and 360.
72. Bradley, op. cit., 1, p. 17.
73. Maskelyne, J. N., in *Model Railway News,* v. 24, p. 203 (Nov. 1948), emphatically distinguishing it from the Adams green.
74. Collins, J. B. B., in *Railway Magazine,* v. 15, p. 287 (Sept. 1904).
75. *Locomotive Magazine,* v. 2, p. 77 (May 1897).
76. Paint fragments described in Appendix 2.1.
77. Colour plate in *Railway and Travel Monthly,* v. 2, f.p. 440 (May 1911).
78. Matched from sample panels prepared during the 1948 restoration of no. 563 (HMRS archives).
79. Matched from similar sample panel to that of ref. 78, in Mr. B. I. Fletcher's collection.
80. Ellis, *SWR,* coloured frontispiece.
81. Ellis, C. H., *The Beauty of Old Trains,* London, George Allen and Unwin, 1952, coloured frontispiece.
82. Ellis, *SWR,* coloured plate f.p. 64.
83. Ellis, *SWR,* p. 217.
84. Nock, O. S., *The London and South-Western Railway,* London, Ian Allan, 1965, p. 98.
85. Matched from model by Basset-Lowke Ltd. (M7 0-4-4T purchased new in 1916 and not repainted since) in Mr. J. F. Parker's collection.
86. Cooper, B. K., in *Railway Magazine,* v. 78, pp. 1-4 (Jan. 1936).
87. Goodway, C. A., in *South Western Circular,* no. 16, pp. 120-4 (Summer 1968) and no. 17, p. 139 (Autumn 1968).
88. L S W R, *Specification of four-wheels coupled Bogie Engine,* Feb. 1898, (the specification for class C8 engines issued to Messrs. Dübs), details extracted by Mr. K. O'B. Nichols.
89. *Locomotive Magazine,* v. 13, p. 156 (14th Sep. 1907).
90. Ellis, *SWR,* p. 167.
91. Collins, in op. cit., p. 285.
92. Goodway, C. A., in *Model Railway Constructor,* v. 35, p. 135 (Apr. 1968).
93. Bradley, op. cit., 2, p. 108.
94. Goodway, C. A., in *South Western Circular,* no. 3, pp. 11-12 (Spring 1965).
95. Such an additional band was a feature of Drummond's C R livery (see *HMRS Livery Register no. 1,* p. 5). In a private communication, Mr D. Burton has remarked on the similarity between the C R and L S W R schemes in this respect, and recorded his belief, based on youthful conversations with old railwaymen, that the extra C R colour was not deep Prussian blue but crimson lake, as used on the valances.
96. Bradley, op. cit., 2, p. 70.
97. Ibid., p. 107.
98. Burtt, op. cit., p. 36.
99. Bradley, op. cit., 2, p. 114.
100. *HMRS Livery Register no. 1,* f.p. 8.
101. Thanks are due to the Editor of the *Railway Observer* for publishing an appeal for details. Bradley, op. cit., 1, p. 17 records that some plates went abroad; perhaps one exists still in the Far East.
102. Goodway, C. A., in *Model Railway News,* v. 41, p. 39 (Jan. 1965).
103. Transfer on modern panel in Mr. N. Pattenden's collection. For colours see reproduction of the arms in Nock, O.S., *Steam Railways of Britain in Colour,* London, Blandford, 1967, pp. 58, 147.

104. Rhodes, M., private communication of measurements of lettering visible on tender no. DS 3001 (ex K10 no. 146, ex L11 no. 159, ex T9 no. 283, and thus probably built in late 1899 (Bradley, op. cit., 2, pp. 99, 129, 132)).
105. Photo in *Railway Magazine,* v. 24, p. 197 (March 1909).
106. Girod-Eymery, H., private communication. Note also the model of an Ouest Railway 4-6-0 of 1901 in the Science Museum (exhibit no. 1903/9).
107. Ellis, C. H., *Four Main Lines,* London, George Allen and Unwin, 1950, p. 211.
108. Gaywood, M., in *Railway Modeller,* v. 20, p. 313 (Oct. 1969).
109. Source not known, note via Mr. K. O'B. Nichols.
110. Jackson, G. G., *All about our British Railways,* London, T.C. and E. C. Jack, 1922, p. 20.
111. Howard Turner, J.T., colour from his contemporary model, matched to prototype in good condition.
112. Paint fragments described in Appendix 2.7.
113. There is even less firm evidence about the minor colours of the Urie livery than about the basic colour.
114. Howard Turner, J.T., private communication of recollections.
115. Carter, op. cit., p. 325.
116. Allen, P. C., and MacLeod, A. B., *Rails in the Isle of Wight,* London, George Allen and Unwin 1967, p.26.
117. ibid., p. 51, also Maskelyne, J. N., quoted by Gough, R. J., in *Railway Modeller* v. 21, p. 58 (Feb. 1970).
118. Carter, op. cit., p. 326.
119. Nunn, K. A. C. R., in *Stephenson Locomotive Society Journal,* (March 1943).
120. S R drawing no. 6654 dated 9th Jan. 1926, class U 2-6-0.
121. Fletcher, B. I., private communication of transcript of document issued from Ashford in Nov. 1923, seen at Ryde works.
122. Sedgwick, A., in *Railway Modeller,* v. 20, p. 244 (Aug. 1969).
123. Matched from model of G C R locomotive smokebox, exhibit no. 1945/32 in the Science Museum, South Kensington.
124. Kerr, A. F. J., in *Railway Modeller,* v. 20, p. 313 (Oct. 1969).
125. Blackburn, A., private communication.
126. Colour from paint sample supplied from Ashford works in 1929 to Mr. S. B. Dent; includes one coat of clear varnish on the green only.
127. Sedgwick, A. private communication of his view and that of acquaintances in the Southampton area who also remembered the colour.
128. Colour from paint produced in c. 1960 by Messrs. Bond's; includes one coat of clear varnish.
129. Sedgwick, A., colour produced to the satisfaction of those mentioned in note 127.
130. Secretan, M., colour plate in *Railway Magazine,* v. 78, f.p. 1.
131. Tustin, R. E., private communication of recollections.
132. Bradley, op. cit., 2, p. 134.
133. Ibid., 2, p. 187.
134. Carter, op. cit., p. 327, re engine no. 850 *Lord Nelson.*
135. Shelley, H. A., private communication of recollections.
136. Bradley, op. cit., 2, p. 155.
137. In *Railway Magazine,* v. 24, p. 187 (March 1909).
138. Hutchings, R. S., *Manual of Decorated Type Faces,* London, Cary Adams and Mackay, 1965, p. 44.
139. See for example photographs in Winstone, R., *Bristol as it was 1914-1900* (*sic*), Bristol, the Author, 1957, figs. 62, 76.
140. Photograph in ibid., fig. 53.
141. Fletcher, B. I., private communication of measurements taken from tender of 0-6-0 no. 32450 in 1950.
142. S R drawing no. A 5924, *Southern and Number Diagram for Locos,* (undated).
143. Chatham, P., from study of photographs.
144. Brackenborough, A. T., in *Railway Modeller,* v. 20, pp. 152-3 (May 1969).
145. Tustin, R. E., from study of photographs.
146. Measurements and details from a transfer in Mr. B. I. Fletcher's collection.
147. Bradley, op. cit., 2, p. 39.
148. S R drawing nos. 3565, 3567, (painting details for H16 4-6-2T and Adams 0-6-0).
149. Fletcher, B. I., from examination of photographs.
150. Drawn from a plate in the collection of Mr. A. R. Brown.
151. Bradley, op. cit., 2, p. 179.
152. S R drawings nos. A 6499 and A 6526, relating to "River" class engines.
153. S R drawing no. A 6766.
154. Drawn from a plate in Mr. Fletcher's collection.
155. Drawn from rubbings obtained by Mr. I. D. Beale.
156. Bradley, op. cit., 1, p. 18.
157. S R drawing no. 3619 (undated).
158. Sedgwick, A., private communication of details compiled from records kept by himself and J. Fairman (Eastleigh information), notes compiled by D. L. Bradley (Ashford information) and other sources.

159. Fletcher, B. I., private communication of information compiled from various printed, photographic and other sources.
160. Bradley, op. cit., 2, p. 31.
161. Ibid., 2, p. 103.
162. Ibid., 2 p. 55.
163. *Railway Magazine,* v. 76, p. 295 (Apr. 1935).
164. Ibid., v. 78, p. 232 (March 1936).
165. Fletcher, B. I., colour description noted during conversations at Eastleigh d.o., 1962.
166. Bradley, op. cit., 2, p. 181, and comtempory issues of the *Railway Observer.*
167. Paint fragments described in Appendix 2.9.
168. Direct Dufaycolor photograph reproduced in *Railway Magazine,* v. 83, f.p. 391 (Dec. 1938) of no. 927 *Clifton,* q.v. in table 6.
169. *Railway Magazine,* v. 85, p. 294 (Oct. 1939).
170. Bradley, op. cit., 2, p. 200.
171. Paint fragment described in Appendix 2.6
172. Paint fragment N351-2 from ex-S E C R coach in Departmental use at Bricklayers Arms. Colour overlaid by B R carmine.
173. Paint fragment described in Appendix 2.8.
174. Paint fragment described in Appendix 2.10
175. Colour from sample panel supplied from Eastleigh works in c. 1962 to Mr. B. I. Fletcher, showing *B R coach green no. 11* as used on class USA 0-6-0T engines.
176. Fletcher, B. I., private communication of measurements taken in 1950 from 0-6-0 no. 32022. It is not certain whether the colour on this engine was yellow or gilt.
177. Allan, I., *The ABC of Southern Locomotives,* London, Ian Allan, n.d. but c. 1966, reprint of October 1943 edition, p. 23.
178. Bradley, op. cit., 2, p. 182.
179. *Railway Magazine,* v. 90, p. 29 (Jan. 1942). The letters had first been seen in autumn 1941. See Railway Observer (Oct. 1941).
180. Fletcher, B. I., private communication of measurements taken from 0-6-2T no. 2573 in autumn 1950.
181. Macleod, A. B., drawings in Allan, op. cit., p.8.
182. Allan, op. cit., p. 9.
183. Burridge, F. H. A., *Nameplates of the Southern Locomotives,* Bournemouth, Sydenham & Co., n.d. but c. 1945, p. 24.
184. Photographs in Allan, op. cit., passim.
185. Fletcher, B. I., private communication.
186. Reed, A. J., in *Railway Modeller,* v. 20, p. 153 (May 1969).
187. *Stephenson Locomotive Society Journal,* v. 25, f.p. 249 (Nov. 1949).
188. Photograph in Day-Lewis, S., *Bulleid, Last Giant of Steam,* London, George Allen and Unwin, 1964, f.p. 232.
189. Anwell, B. W., in *Trains Illustrated,* v. 5, p. 7 (Jan. 1952), confirmed by Messrs. S. C. Nash and L. Elsey.
190. Burridge, op. cit., p. 25.
191. Drawing in ibid, p. 14.
192. Drawings in ibid, pp. 8-9.
193. *Railway Observer,* (Dec. 1944).
194. *Design,* no. 171, pp. 72-5 (March 1963).

3.1 The first ten years, 1839-1849.

An extraordinary survival is a panel from what is claimed to be the first railway coach to arrive at Southampton in 1840 [1]. This is so heavily varnished that its original colour is almost indeterminable, but was most likely a very dark brown; the badge of the London and Southampton Railway which it bears is illustrated in fig. 10a. The colours are red and white for the shield and crest, and blue for the garter, with gilt lettering and embellishments shaded with brown.

The panel is arguably from a coach such as those shown in a recently noted lithograph [2]; these are of the common three-bodied type with a two-colour finish — the upper parts of the sides and ends, and the roof, apparently black in the style of a horse-drawn carriage, and the lower parts of a lighter shade. A second lithograph [3] shows three-compartment coaches with a badge on each door, and this agrees with the livery described by Ellis, viz:

Colour:

Chocolate [4, 5]
Dark brown [6]

The coaches were one colour all over with the L S W R coat of arms on the centre door and crests on the outer doors of the first class (only?) [4, 5] — a scheme notably similar to contemporary G W R practice.

A slightly later engraving [7], of about 1850, shows more three-bodied coaches with a two-coloured finish of the more familiar sort, i.e. light-coloured above the (undulating) waist-line and dark below. However the drawing is not very good and the train is merely shown as part of the landscape.

3.2 The L S W R Royal saloon of 1843 [8] is recorded as having been coloured dark maroon [9].

3.3 Approximately from 1855 to 1865, i.e. the time of Joseph Beattie [10].

Colour:

Varnished teak [4, 10, 11]
Varnished mahogany [10, 12]

The varnish was relieved only by the vehicle number in a blue and gold garter design on the lower panel of the middle (?) door (fig. 10b). This description is believed to apply to a first-class coach and is obtained from study of a contemporary painting [11], which additionally shows green curtains. There is no class designation shown, but Ellis, in one of his paintings [13] shows a varnished coach with a true coat of arms on the door and the word SECOND in the waist panel between the doors.

3.4 A cheaper version of the above scheme, probably about 1865.

Colours:

A:	**Moderate brown**	**7·5 YR 4/5 ★10** [14]
B:	Light yellowish pink	7·5 YR 9/4 [14]

Colour A was the external colour, apparently a substitute for varnishing, and colour B was used inside; it probably represents a grained finish.

3.5 An inconclusive two-colour livery

Colours:

A:	**Dark brown** [6, 12]	
	Brown [10]	
	Dark olive green or brown [4]	
	(Olive gray	7·5 Y 3/1) [13]
B.	**Dark cream** [4, 6, 10]	
	Greenish yellow [4, 2]	
	Yellow chrome [6]	
	Yellow [12, 15]	
	(Strong greenish yellow	7·5 Y 8/10 est.) [13]
	(Moderate greenish yellow	7·5 Y 7/7 est.) [13]
C:	Vermilion [10, 12, 16]	
	Scarlet [4]	

This was a conventional two-colour livery with light-coloured upper (and waist [13]) panels. Probably these were varnished white like the first G W R ones. Ellis suggests that they were adopted in imitation of the G W R after the opening to Exeter in 1860 [6]; if so the date of the change was presumably after 1864, the year in which the G W R adopted light-coloured upper panels [17]. The ends of brake vans were bright red [4, 10, 12, 15], a practice dating at least from the Egham accident, which was also in 1864 [16].

3.6 The emergence of the standard scheme of the late 19th century, from c. 1874 to 1885.

Examination of the paint samples described in Appendix 2.2, which are from one of the antique coaches which Ellis records as having been in use around Bournemouth in the 1890s [18], showed that its first repaint included a colour which, while a good deal lighter than the later versions of "salmon", was at least nearer red than yellow. The date of c. 1874 given in the Appendix depends, it should be noted, entirely on the assumptions about frequency of repainting which are set out there and in Appendix 2.5. Ellis suggests that "salmon" may have appeared at the end of the 1870s, having been copied from the S E R [19], but an earlier writer [4] suggests that the salmon and brown scheme existed "from a comparatively early period".

Colours:

A:	Dark brown [6]	
	Brownish gray	**10 YR 3/1** to 2·5 Y 3/1 [14]
B:	Salmon [6]	
	Moderate orange	**2·5 YR 7/6** [14]
	Moderate yellowish pink	10 R 8/4 [14]
C:	Vermilion [10]	
D:	Light yellowish pink	7·5 YR 9/4 [14]

The lower panels of the sides were colour A and the upper panels colour B [6]. The coach ends were brown unless there were horizontal mouldings on them at waist level, when the upper panels seem to have been salmon and the mouldings brown [14], a feature which reappeared on the 1905 rail motors and may have been used at other times. Brake ends were vermilion as before [10, 16], fillets around quarter lights were varnished teak [20] and a coat of arms in a garter was called for on the middle door of second-class coaches at least [20] — a common factor with Adams' 1879 locomotive livery. No certain details of lining have been gleaned.

Interiors were, in the first class, varnished mahogany &c. with ceiling mouldings and the reveals in partitions gilt [21], in the second class varnished mahogany with blue American cloth door panels [20], and in the third class a painted finish in light yellowish pink, possibly changing to white or a grained finish after c. 1882 [14].

3.7 Experimental green liveries, c. 1885.

There are several references in print to coaches having been painted green in the 1880s. Ellis records Mr. Wickham Legg as recalling an apparently green bogie coach at Winchester in 1880 or 1881, and also Mr. Frank Box's recollection of seeing a train of dark green coaches at Richmond [22, 23]. A similar train was remarked by Mr. Bushell in 1884 or 1885 [24]. These latter observations are almost certainly connected with events recorded in the Minutes of the L S W R Locomotive and Stores Committee in 1885. On 5th August there occurs the entry " . . . a block train to be painted the same colour as the Directors' new inspection coach" (the 46 ft. saloon which later became DS 1 under British Railways' ownership) and on 28th August Mr. Adams reported that " ... a block train of the same colour [as the engines which had recently been painted green] is now working on the Leatherhead line" [25]. Although this seems to mean the familiar Adams pea green which had just been introduced, the Company's house magazine was explicit that the colour was dark green and suggested that gilt lining would be an improvement. The train was identified as block train no. 3 [26] and by the coincidence that it had suffered a coupling failure in the previous year, the coaches which comprised it can be identified [27] as follows:

3rd brake no. 368 (built 1873, 25 ft. 0 in. x 8 ft. 0 in., broken up Dec. 1901); 3rd no. 356 (built 1873, 23 ft. 8 in. x 8 ft. 0 in., broken up Dec. 1901); 2nd no. 98; composite no. 102; 1st no. 466; 1st no. 468; 1st no. 470; 1st no. 467; composite no. 15 (built 1871, 2 - 1 - 1 - 2, 24 ft. 0 in. x 8 ft. 0 in., broken up Dec. 1901); 2nd no. 117; 3rd no. 355; 3rd brake no. 367.

3.8 The salmon and brown livery in the years 1885-1906.

The limits of this period have been chosen to comprise the greater part of the working life of the flat-roofed four-wheeled coaches.

Colours:

A: Moderate reddish brown
  2·5 YR 3/3 [28]
  Dark grayish brown 5 YR 2/2 [28, 29]
  Brownish gray **10 YR 3/1** [14] ★ 12
  Brownish gray 2·5 Y 3/1 [14]

B: Moderate yellowish pink
  2·5 YR 7/5 [29]
  Moderate orange
  2·5 YR 7/6 [14, 28] ★ 11
  Moderate yellowish pink
  2·5 YR 8/4 [28]
  Light yellowish pink 2·5 YR 9/3 [28]
  Brownish orange 5 YR 5/8 [30, 31]
  Moderate yellowish pink
  5 YR 8/4 [28, 29]
  Light orange 5 YR 8/7 [31]

C: **Vivid red** **7·5 R 3·5/16** [30]

D: Strong yellowish brown
  7·5 YR 5/6 [30]

E: *Light oak*
  Moderate yellowish pink
  2·5 YR 8/4 [14]
  Pale orange yellow 7·5 YR 8·5/4 [30]

The livery can be more exactly described in this period. The upper panels of the sides (including the waist panel) were again salmon, and the lower parts of the sides, the cantrail, ends and probably also the underframe, bogies and wheels were dark brown [32]. The ends, and probably also the headstocks and buffer guides, of brake vans were red at first [30], but this was quickly dispensed with as soon as the vacuum brake (or pipes) had been fitted to all the working passenger stock. This was reported to the Committee on 9th November 1887 [33], and Mr. Panter was authorised to discontinue the practice of painting the ends of guards' vans vermilion (n.b.) on 9th May 1888 [34]. The painting details of cabooses* are not known for certain, but a general colour of dark brown seems likely. Roofs and wheel rims were white ex factory [32]. Roof fittings were black [32]. Lining, lettering and class designations seem to have been similar to later practice except that the vehicle number seems more often to have appeared once only on each side [32, 35] and the railway's initials appeared as L & S W R until about the turn of the century [36]. Painting details appropriate to the period 1885-1906 are given in figs. 10c, d, 11a, f, [36], 10e [37], 10f [38], 12a [39], 12b, c, e, f, h [40]. Lettering was in gold leaf and black paint [36]. Labels designating smoking and ladies only compartments were etched into the window glass, originally in the light on the hinge side of the door, but in coaches built from 1904 onwards, on the handle side (see figs. 11b, 13j).

Interior colouring seems to have been much as before. In the third class, the walls above the waist-line were moderate yellowish pink [14], and the ceilings of third-class coaches [14] and of vans [30] were white. Van interiors were plain as well; successively white, strong yellowish brown (c. 1889) and moderate orange [30].

3.9 A special scheme for ambulance trains produced in 1900 [41].

Upper panels of sides	French grey
Lower panels of sides, and fascias	Khaki

Lining of panels in yellow and red (this was presumably carried out in the style used for rail motor cars — see section 3.11). Small Geneva crosses and Royal arms were applied.

3.10 Edwardian times and after — the salmon and brown livery.

In the period covered by this section and those following, coach liveries gave rise to many conflicting descriptions. Besides the variability or

*Caboose: I am indebted to Mr. J. T. Howard Turner for the information that this was the name in use amongst L S W R staff for a roof-top lookout. The etymology appears to be nautical — see *O.E.D.*

subtlety of "salmon", which has taxed the powers of witnesses and imitators for half a century, direct contradictions have arisen over the colours used for the lower panels of coach sides. Although a recent attempt to produce salmon colour from its ingredients (see Appendices 1.10 and 1.21) did not produce an absolute match with surviving specimens [42], it did allow attention to be turned to the alleged green shade of the lower panels. It became clear that no easily available green pigment could be used in the recipe quoted in Appendix 1.6 to result in a visibly brown shade. This conclusion was however in such flat contradiction of other evidence that discussion tended to stalemate. But clarification was given by Mr. D. W. Knight, who drew on the recollections of two members of his family, who knew or worked on the L S W R. It appeared that, from the time of the introduction of corridor coaches (i.e. from 1904), the original dark brown colouring was replaced by an indeterminate shade which ranged from very dark brown to very dark green, sometimes appearing almost black (suggestive of pickled walnuts). This "colour" lasted until about the end of the 1914-18 war, when the old dark brown reappeared. Mr. Knight adds that the range of shades of this too was legion [43].

The colour shades which are listed below are all believed to date from this period, although many are impressions recollected after a period of many years, and it does appear possible to divide them rationally into two categories, A1 consisting of those which appear to refer to an identifiably brown shade, and A2 comprising the others. But comparision with Section 3.8 shows that the suggestion of a new colour having been introduced c. 1904 cannot be correct; it looks as though two varieties of the main colour had been in use from at least 1890.

As for "salmon" it is sufficient to say that none of the samples examined has been of a colour which would immediately be called pink, and in this respect the epithet is likely to mislead a modern reader. But the samples give ground for thinking that there was a tendency for the colour to be made more dark and intense after about 1900; this is shown in the diagram in Appendix 3. A note on the traditional use of the colour name is included in Appendix 1.9.

Many vehicles retained their pre-war finish until well after the grouping; one, no. 073S, until as late as 1931 [44]. Since this implies that they went without repainting for ten years or more, some pretty shabby and discoloured liveries were probably to be seen. It is interesting to note in this connexion that only one substantial paint sample seems to survive of L S W R salmon and brown underlying an S R paint system; the S R seem usually to have cleaned the body down to a bare carcass.

Colours:

A1: *Purple brown* [44]
Dark brown [10]
Chocolate [45]
Very dark chocolate [46]
Worcester sauce brown [47]
Dark umber becoming grey-black [48]
Moderate brown, colour no. 3-045 of BS 2660 : 1955 — 7·5 YR 3·5/4 [43]
Dark grayish yellowish brown, no. 3-038 of BS 2660 : 1955 — 10 YR 3/2 [43]
Dark grayish reddish brown — **2·5 YR 2/2** [31, 49]
Dark grayish brown — **5 YR 2/2 est.** [49]
(*Dark brown*) [50]
(Moderate reddish brown — 2·5 YR 3/3) [51]
(Dark brown, colour no. 3-039 of BS 2660 : 1955 — 5 YR 1·5/4) [52]
(Dark yellowish brown — 10 YR 1/2 est.) [53]

A2: Body brown — Appendix 1.7
Dark brown — Appendix 1.6
Very dark greenish brown [54]
Black [55]
"Not black really, but a sort of off-black, but it depends how you look at it" [56]
Grey-black [48]
Brownish gray — **2·5 Y 3/1** [14] ★ 12
Black — — [49]
(Brownish black — 2·5 YR 1/1 est.) [57, 58]
(Grayish olive, no. 641 of BS 381C : 1964 — 10 Y 3/1·5) [59]

B: *Salmon pink* [44] — Appendices 1.9 and 1.10
Salmon brown — Appendices 1.11 and 1.12
Tan [44]
Warm stone [46, 50]
Orangish salmon [47]
Shrimp pink [60]
Salmon, a light golden brown [6]
Salmon, a golden sand colour [61]
Brownish pink, growing browner with age [10]
Orange yellow [45]
Yellow buff with a pink tone [58]
Light buff which was pinkish when new [43]
Moderate yellowish pink, no. 2-030 of BS 2660 : 1955 — 5 YR 8/4 [43]
Brownish orange — **5 YR 5/8** [30, 31]
Strong orange — **5 YR 6/11** [31]
Grayish reddish orange — 2·5 YR 6/6 est.) [58]
(Moderate orange — 2·5 YR 6/9 est.) [52, 59]
(Strong brown — 2·5 YR 4·5/5 est.) [53]
(Strong brown, Carter's no. 48 — 2·5 YR 4·5/5 est.) [62]
(Strong brown, no. 3-044 of BS 2660 : 1955 — 5 YR 4·5/6) [52]
(Moderate orange, no. 2-031 of BS 2660 : 1955 — 2·5 YR 7/6) [57]
repainted to
(Brownish orange — 5 YR 5/8) [57]
discoloured to
(Strong brown — 5 YR 4/5) [57]

A2+B: Black and tan [44]

C: *Lining brown* — Appendix 1.8
Dark brown [46, 63]
Black [49]
Dark grayish reddish brown — **2·5 YR 2/2** [31]
(*Dark brown*) [52]
(Black [6, 53]

D: *Lining red* — Appendix 1.13
Red [58]
Vermilion [46, 63]
Deep reddish orange — **7·5 R 4/11** [31]

E: Lemon yellow [10, 64]

F: *Mahogany* [65]
Dull red, faded to a shade similar to red

oxide [66]

A colour which faded to a light reddish brown [67]

Effectively dark brown [43]

Grayish red **7·5 R 4/6** est. [31]

(Dark reddish brown 7·5 R 2/4 est.) [57]

Surrey Warner's own description of paint shop practice was as follows [65]:

> The upper portion of the coach should receive three coats of top colour and one coat of varnish top colour, the lower parts and ends to receive two coats of lead colour, one of brown and one of varnish colour. The body can then be picked out with dark brown and fine lined in red, and the quarter light mouldings finished mahogany colour. The writing to be gold with a black shading line, and the whole surface given one coat of first coating varnish and two coats of elastic finishing varnish, flatting down to take place between coats.
>
> Carriage underframes (steel). One coat of anti-corrosive paint and one of lead colour. Solebars and headstocks to be filled in and rubbed down. Then one coat of lead colour, one coat brown and one coat varnish brown.
>
> Roof after canvas is applied receives three coats of white paint.

The expression "upper panels" included clerestories, but the cantrail was brown [40]. Roof fittings were not consistent, either white or black being used; the latter seems to have been more common in service [40]. Drop light frames were mahogany to match the quarter lights [57], and the gas valve cover was red [48]. Wheel tyres were as usual white ex factory.

Up to the 1912 renumbering the general size of all lettering was 2½ in. high over the gilt part, plus about ½ in. of black shading, although initials of words, but not the railway's own initials, were up to 3 in. high. GUARDS was written without an apostrophe, and so was COMPT. Examples of the layout of lettering in this period are shown in figs. 10h [30, 35], j, 12g, j, k [35]. After 1912 the basic size for the number and the railway's initials was altered to approximately 4 in. high, and instead of being spaced out along the vehicle's length the two items were placed together in one panel near the centre of the vehicle as shown in fig. 12. l. Dining saloons had successively 4 in. (1904) and 6 in. (1907) company initials, and Royal vehicles (of which the kitchen brake shown in fig. 12k was one) had letters of approximately 3¼ in. The placing of the number in the waist panel of a lookout was frequent on brake vans; in these cases the initials were usually above the number — the converse of fig. 12. l [40]. The style of the numbers was similar to but more regular than the locomotive type shown in fig. 2f.

Class designations were usually spelt out, but the 1903 bogie block trains had 12 in., apparently gilt, numbers on the doors (fig. 13d) although these were superseded by 1ST, 2ND, 3RD in the waist panel by 1910 at latest (see fig. 13e) [68].

Lining was applied to the sides as shown in fig. 11b in colours C and D. It comprised six complete loops per full-size compartment, together with one line under the waist moulding and possibly another along the top of the moulding forming the lower edge of the side. There does not seem to have been lining along the cantrail or on the ends. Although the colour for the curved part of the mouldings was officially body brown, it seems often to have appeared black and thus distinct from the colour of the lower panels [58]. During the 1914-18 war, some old third-class coaches appear not to have been lined out [35], and later some four-wheel passenger luggage vans had only white lining [58].

Set numbers were marked in white [69] on the ends of end vehicles (as in figs. 13g, h) — where numbers less than ten were prefixed by "NO." [35] — and on the left hand end of the solebars of each coach, in approximate two-inch figures.

"Smoking" notices were etched on the window panes as before (the letters were clear glass; fig. 13j is drawn as a negative). Toilet windows were also decoratively etched; in the gangwayed stock of 1904-08 they incorporated a monogram of the Company's initials.

Compartment door interiors showed the class designations in words (fig. 13a, b) [14, 57] or figures (fig. 13c) [68], probably always matching the inscription outside. Plain black letters were the rule in thirds; the coach number was also marked on the door in about 2 in. figures, but its position varied [14, 57, 70]. Higher class compartments had gilt wording shaded with black to left, and the coach number to the right of the window strap [70].

Internal woodwork was of varying material and finish according to the class of accommodation: oak, walnut and Hungarian ash in the first class, plywood and mahogany in the second and grained and varnished deal in the third and in vans [30, 71]. Corridors were usually faced with mahogany and plywood although some 1904 composite coaches had white-painted panelling above the waist. Ceilings were always white, lined out in gold for the first class, chocolate brown for the second class and pink for the third [71]. The inside window frames in the first class (only [40, 58]) were painted lemon yellow so that they could be easily located from the platform [10, 64]. Upholstery was in blue cloth in the first class [58, 64], complemented by a blue mat incorporating the Company's initials [71, 72], and gold trimmings [64]. Second class upholstery was in golden brown plush [64] and third class, red and black moquette or rep [48, 58]. Corridor handrails were of polished brass [71].

3.11 Steam rail motors.

The livery of these vehicles was settled when Drummond's inspection engine no. 733 came out in 1899. From the paint samples obtained from the saloon portion of this engine and described in Appendix 2.1, it is apparent that it was first painted entirely as a locomotive, i.e. in green, and only later as a hybrid. Probably to give an effect to the panelling balancing that of the engine part, the saloon later had all the mouldings on the sides and end picked out in dark brown and lined in the distinctly ornate combination of red and gilt (fig. 11k). The upper and waist panels were salmon and the lower panels chocolate brown, with a conventional number and coat of arms on them respectively [31, 73, 74, 75]. False louvres were painted on the side ventilators [75]. This was incidentally the first Drummond engine without a number plate.

When the first two "steam motor cars" came out in 1903, they bore this same livery (fig. 11f), except for the small details that all the lettering was in a special style of gilt with a narrow black border all round each letter and that there was no coat of arms [40]. Burtt notes that these two cars, operated jointly with the L B S C R on the Fratton-Southsea branch, were soon repainted in Brighton colours as to their saloon portions [76], but Bradley stated that only Joint no. 1 was so treated [77]. The difference would be small; one coat of paint on the upper panels.

The later cars for the Basingstoke and Alton Light Railway (L S W R nos. 1 and 2) were also treated as complete trains from the paint-shop point of view, and the engine compartment and underframes were coloured and picked out in green and purple brown, while the coach portion was again painted in brown and salmon with brown mouldings [35, 78]. The later series of all-enclosed cars, nos. 3-15 of 1905-6, were painted entirely as carriages except in having red buffer beams with *shaded* gilt numbers on them [35], and green wheels and cylinder casings [78].

Once established, this tram-like livery was continued for trailer cars having driving compartments; these also had the blank end painted salmon and brown [35].

3.12 Ventilated milk vans.

Some of the 32 ft. six-wheel type with sliding doors were painted salmon all over the sides and ends when new in 1907, to keep them cool in hot weather. The usual lining of (effectively) black and red was applied around each panel [35]. The floors of these vans were of asphalt and internal painting was in white [79]. The lettering conformed to contemporary practice: the number appeared twice, and the initials L S W R once, in the waist panels, while the words MILK VAN were placed in the middle of the main upper panels between the doors. Grey slate panels seem to have been incorporated in the waist-line of the doors for the chalking of loading instructions [35].

3.13 Other coaching stock vans.

These were painted plain brown. Although Ellis describes this colour as "very dark umber" and implies that it was the same colour as that used for goods wagons [80], the paint samples described in Appendix 2.2 show that this old coach was painted brownish gray all over, i.e. the passenger coach body brown. This conclusion agrees with a statement by Mr. Tustin [81], who also says that gilt lettering was applied to horse boxes, and grouped on the drop flap. This arrangement, with the Company initials above the number, seems to have been usual, although the size of the lettering seems to have varied a great deal, from about 2½ in. [68] to 7 in. [35] on different sorts of covered vans. Open carriage trucks however had the initials in the centre and the number at both ends, as for an actual coach. Coaches adapted as fruit vans were not repainted, but some had the word FRUIT marked on the solebars under the partition at the left-hand end, in a size of about 3½ in. to 4 in. [40]. They were formed into set trains which carried numbers in the usual locations — on the ends of the brake coaches and at the left end of the solebars, e.g. F 17 [40].

3.14 The sage green scheme.

This colour was introduced for the first electric stock in 1915 and was probably intended to be the same as that used on locomotives during the latter part of the war period (see Section 2.10 After the war, the scheme was extended to the London suburban six-wheelers used for race traffic, and officially from March 1921 to all other coaches [82]. Probably the enforced economy of the war years was the cause of the change, but the selection of the new colour was surely influenced by foreign practice. Several instances of the adoption of features of American liveries occurred in the years before the war, when a succession of British engineers visited the U.S.A. and Canada, and the introduction of the L S W R electric trains had followed the visit of that railway's Electrical Engineer to the States [83]. But it is interesting to note the possibility of French influence also. At the time of introducing its new livery, the L S W R was the only main line company in England to use a green finish. Second class, it may be noted, was abolished on 22nd July 1918.

Colours:

A: *Sage green* [84]
Green [82]
Sage green, similiar to the locomotives or perhaps lighter [43]
Engine-green [85]
Dark sage green . . . weathered badly [86]
(Grayish olive, no. 641 of BS 381C: 1964 10 Y 3/1·5 (near)) [58]★13
Grayish olive green 5 GY 3/2 [49] discoloured to
Grayish olive green 2·5 GY 3/1 [49]
Moderate olive green 5 GY 4/3 [49]
Moderate olive green, no. 5-065 of BS 2660 : 1955 5 GY 4/6 [87] ★ 14
n.b. the leaves of the sage herb have a colour of approximately 5 GY 5/4

B1: *Yellow* [82]
Orange chrome [86]
Gilt [58, 88]

B2: Gilt [86, 88]

C: Black [86, 88]

It appears that the original scheme merely substituted green for the browns of the previous livery (see section 3.10), for some paint samples (Appendices 2.6.2 and 2.6.3) suggest that body ends and solebars were painted green. Some photographs also suggest a light colour on solebars and bogies. However, Mr. Tustin remarks [89] that to the best of his knowledge he never saw any green solebars, and he was in the habit of taking note of details which were marked thereon, such as set numbers. Mr. Howard Turner confirms [58] that underframes and ends were black, and it seems likely that green paint in these locations was either an undercoat or a short-lived feature. The anticipated life of this livery was five years between repaints [90].

Lining was applied only to the sides (but the driving ends of electric trains counted as "sides"). Its colouring, B1 and C, has been reported as gold and black, but bearing in mind the ambiguity of the word "gold" as applied to colour descriptions, it is not surprising to find that in fact the lines were yellow and black as in Southern days. This is confirmed by a note in the Board minutes of 17th March 1921 that "green colour with yellow lines shall be adopted for all the Company's coaching stock" [82], and also by Surrey Warner himself [91]. But transfers of lettering were almost equally certain to have been gilt and black as previously. Some of the wording was however dispensed with — see fig. 12d which represents a 30 ft. brake van [35]. The change of lining colour allowed an extra band of lining to be seen [35] running along the top edge of the moulding at floor level of the electric sets (see fig. 11b), and it is likely that this was also present in the salmon and brown scheme. Other details of steam stock continued to be coloured as noted in section 3.10, but the electric sets had grey roofs [35], and numbers in a series E1-84 [88] marked in 4 in. transfers above the route stencil holders on the driving ends [35].

The interiors of steam stock continued to be as listed in section 3.10; in electric stock the ceilings were white and the woodwork varnished dark [58]. In the first class the upholstery was plain dark blue [58, 83] and in the third class, red and black tapestry [83] or sometimes brown leather [58].

3.15 Horse boxes and other van stock.

Generally as described in section 3.14, with lining on panelled stock [35]. The lettering indicated on Mr. Tustin's drawing [81] of the horse boxes with "L S W R" above the number on the drop flap, was removed to the groom's door and consequently reduced in size [35].

3.16 Southern Railway coaches, 1923-38.

The S R coach livery was a direct continuation of the final L S W R scheme, and evidence printed in Appendix 2 confirms the frequently-made statement that the S R originally used the same basic green colour as had the L S W R.

Colours:

A1: Green, similar to the L S W R shade [43]
Grayish olive green
5 GY 3/2 [31, 92]
Moderate olive green
5 GY 3/3 est. [93]
Moderate olive green
5 GY 4/3 [94]
Moderate olive green
5 GY 4/6 [31, 87] ★ 14
Moderate olive green
7.5 GY 4/4 [31]

A2: *Olive green* Appendix 1.14
Moderate olive green
2·5 GY 3/3 [95, 96, 97] ★ 5
Dark grayish green
10 GY 3/2 [87]
Dark yellowish green
2.5 G 3/3 [49]
(Moderate olive green, Carter's no. 21,
5 GY 3/6 (near)) [62]
n.b., colour before varnishing approximately
Grayish olive green
2.5 GY 4/1 [95]

B: *Yellow* [98]
Primrose [81]
Primrose . . . rather pale to start with but a rather richer shade was used later on [89]
Golden orange, tended to lose brilliance rather rapidly and took on a more yellowish colour [99]
Moderate yellow 4 Y 8/5 [87]
Strong orange **5 YR 7/11** [95]
Strong orange, no. 0-004 of BS 2660:1955
2.5 YR 7/12 (near) [95]

C: Gilt [89]

D: Black [88]

E1: White, which quickly turned cream and then dirty brown (up to the early 1930s) [89]

E2: Grey (later 1930s) [89]

A semi-official description of the paint shop procedure was published in 1933 [100] and ran:

PAINT AND MORE PAINT

> A man who embarks on the painting of a coach must of necessity be an enthusiast, for between the first and final touch of his brush are no less than twelve coats of paint, excluding the lining and putting on of letters and figures by transfer. As each coat is applied, the coach changes its hue with a rapidity which would bewilder a chameleon. Pink, grey and yellow follow each other in quick succession until, ceasing from this indecisive oscillation, the painters persevere with green. After one coat of varnish, the delicate lining round the panels and corners is done by the experts. The words "SOUTHERN RAILWAY", "GUARD", and the significant numbers "1" and "3" are then put on with gold leaf transfers that add glamour [! — L. T.] to the coach. Two more coats of varnish to preserve the paint and the outside is at last finished.

In contrast to the L S W R specification printed in Section 3.10, which calls for only seven coats of paint and varnish, the S R scheme resembles the G W R scheme of c. 1918 [101] — and perhaps a whole tradition of elaborate paint systems. Perhaps Mr. Warner, who was still advocating the L S W R system in print in 1923 [90] thought that the G W R system he had grown up with was unnecessarily elaborate, or perhaps the L S W R was deliberately economising. At any rate, the S R paint finishes were made to last longer than those of the L S W R, once the original green shade A1 was rejected. That colour used to turn blue when coaches were stored near the sea [89]. The new shade (A2) was introduced not later than 1929 [95], but it is clear that a number of vehicles carried the old colour, or were even repainted in it, well into the 1930s [31, 87, 93, 94]. As noted in Appendix 1.14, the later green also tended to turn blue under some circumstances (although none of the samples examined seems to have suffered); but revarnishing in service darkened it [102].

The sides alone of coaches were green (given the exception that auto-trailers and electrics had green driving ends). Underframes and coach ends were black and roofs were colour E. Lining was applied to the sides in what was basically the L S W R style — even on steel panelled coaches. The style shown in fig. 11d [98] was usual, but square-cornered lining (fig. 11c) was used on ex-L C D R stock with rectangular mouldings, and for

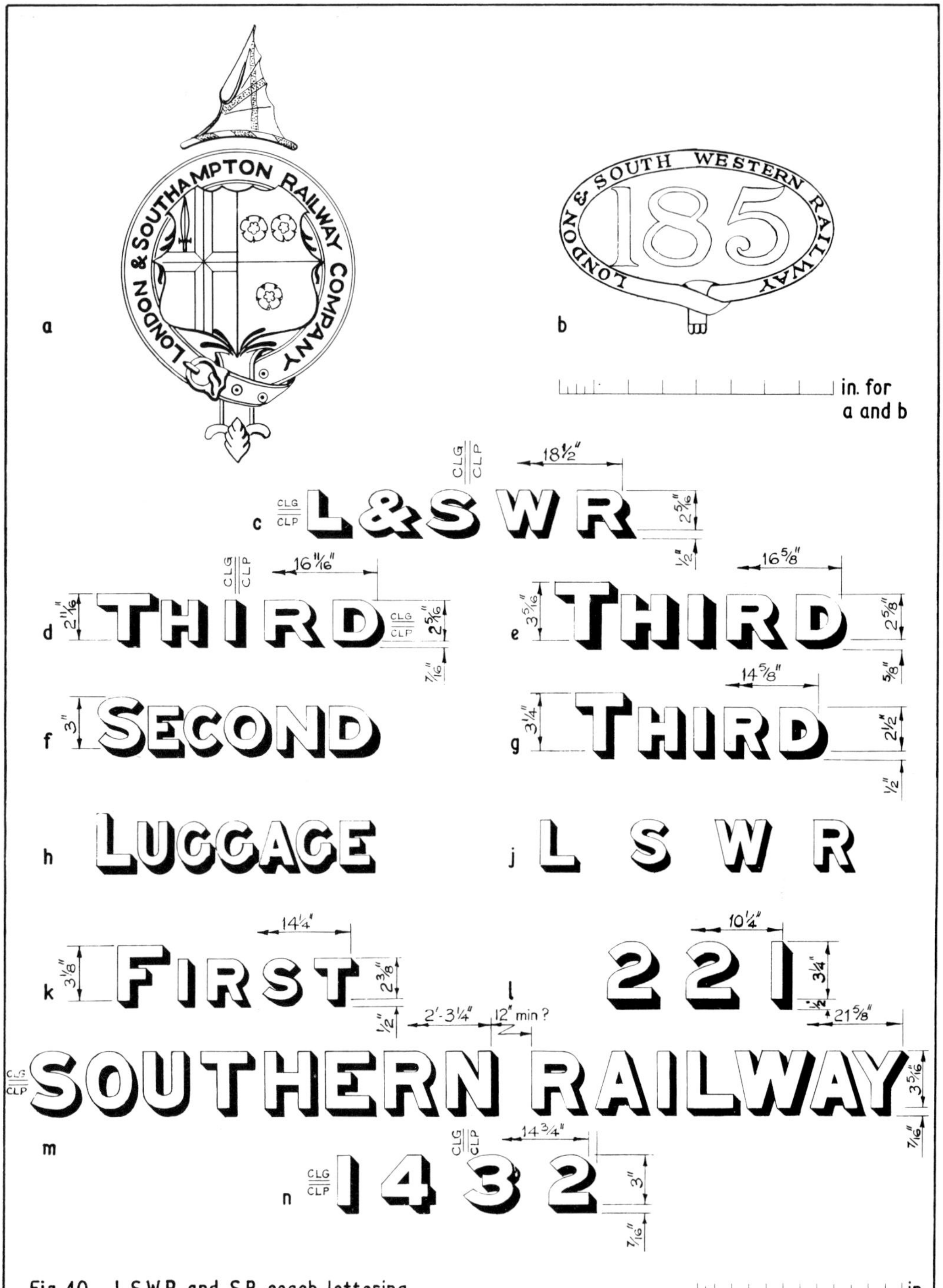

Fig. 10 LSWR and SR coach lettering

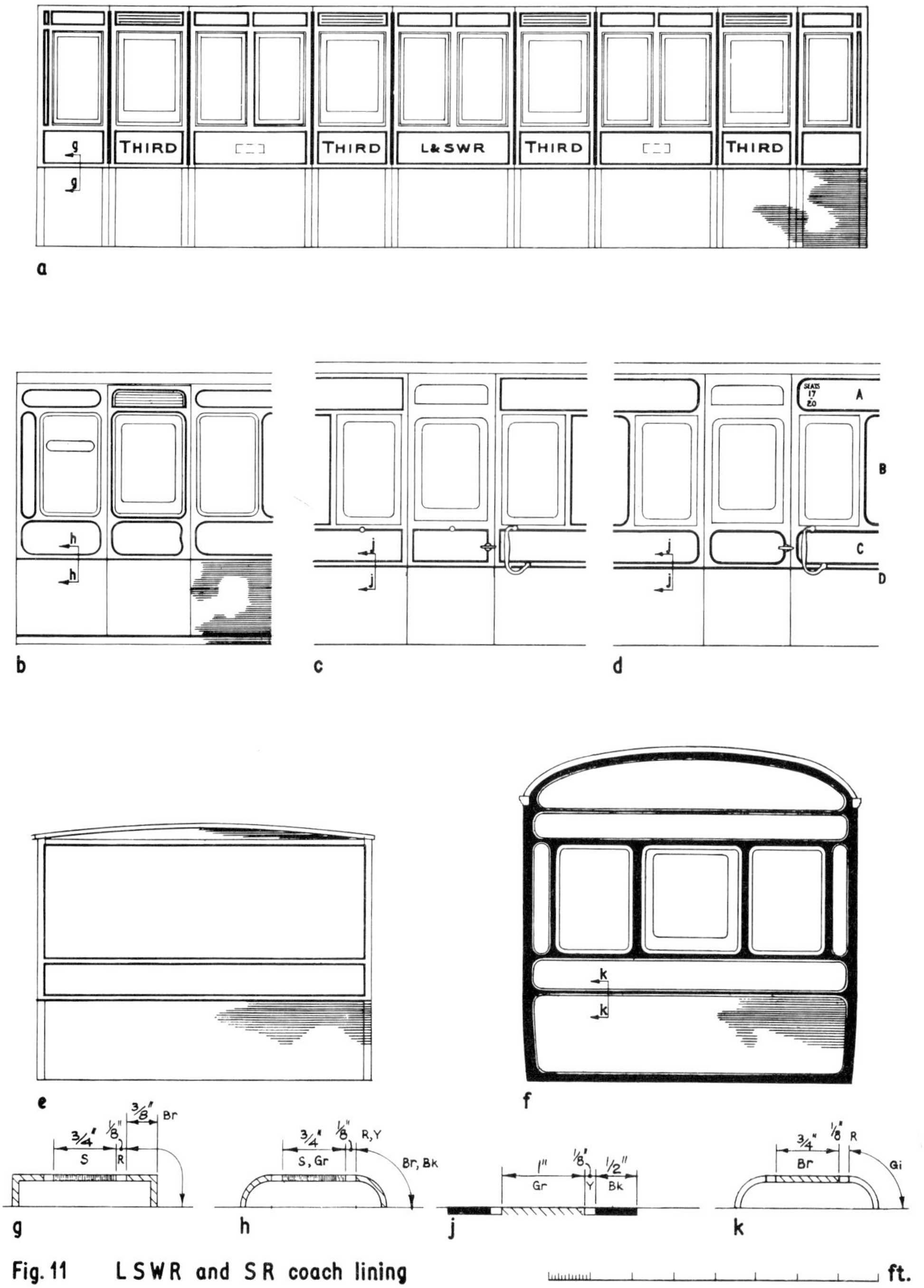

Fig. 11 LSWR and SR coach lining

a while on steel-panelled stock as well [103, 104]. By 1930 it had gone and simplification of the lining was being tried, probably because the old style did not match the construction of the then new deep-windowed stock. Various combinations of the four components of the old lining were tried (see fig. 11d for reference letters, and note that there is no indication that the S R ever applied lining in the lowest position shown in fig. 11b). Thus from c. 1930 A + B + C was usual (but open thirds nos. 1282-1311 had B + D only), in 1936 the second batch of open thirds, nos. 1410-1450 had B + C only, and c. 1937 cars for the first stage Portsmouth electrification scheme had C only [105]

Lettering followed the former L S W R practice in marking the Company title in the centre of the vehicle with the number at both ends. But all these transfers were placed in the cant-rail panel, the words SOUTHERN RAILWAY being placed symmetrically with the centre-line of the vehicle as far as possible, if necessary being separated by a blank panel — and a compartment door or two. But in accordance with the painters' feelings for effect, the letters and numbers were usually arranged so as to be in the centre of the panel as a whole (see figs. 10m, n and 13q [106] and note that "CLP" and "CLG" stand respectively for centre line of panel and centre line of gilding). On deep-windowed stock the company title was perforce marked in the waist panel. Class designations were in words on steam stock (fig. 10k [105], but in figures on electric stock motor coaches and Brighton line pantry coaches [105]. Approximate 7in. figures in the waist panel (fig. 13f [35]) gave way to 9 in. figures in the lower panel. All these letters and numbers, although of similiar appearance to those used by the L S W R, seem in fact to have been drawn out afresh in different sizes. Seat numbers were introduced in the cant-rail panel in this period. The legend for the third-class compartment at the right-hand end of the non-corridor side would be SEATS 1/4 and so on, working towards the left end at the rate of four seats per compartment (cf. current B R practice in internal numbering). First class compartments were similarly numbered, following on from the highest third-class number [105] (see fig. 13s which shows the system in use after the war [35]). The standard legend for double doors was GUARD/LUGGAGE but the early bogie utility vans merely had LUGGAGE applied in gilt transfers (fig. 13m [35]). These vans had originally only the same word in the bottom right corner as had ex-L S W R milk vans in this period [106]. This location was standard for SCENERY and COVCAR vans also [105] and this and other subsidiary lettering such as set numbers (fig. 13p [35]) and distributed load limit, and also dimensions etc, on the data plates on the ends were yellow [107]. To this period, c. 1930 [58] also belongs the introduction by the S R of a conspicuous marking for stove-fitted brake vans; the painting of the end vertical panel of a brake van [107] or a rectangular patch on a utility type [108] in the same bright yellow. In the former case the number showed through on a stripe of green [107].

More conspicuous notices controlling smoking were introduced in the 1930s. Possibly with faulty logic, the notice permitting smoking was red with white lettering and surround (fig. 13k [109]), while the "non-smoking" notice was basically green with white details [58] and was the same size (fig. 131 [35]). These transfers were fixed to the outside of the window.

Interior finish was not markedly different from the late L S W R practice, but the coach number and class designation inside the doors were in gilt and black transfers to match the exterior [112], and van interiors were pale green [43, 87]. Drop lights and other wooden framing of windows were varnished, probably teak [105].

On S R motor trains, the control hoses were painted in colours indicating their function. Viewed on the end of the coach nearest the engine they were from left to right blue (the regulator control), green (the main storage line) and yellow (the back pressure line) [105].

3.17 Coach liveries in the term of office of O. V. S. Bulleid

A bright, malachite green livery was introduced following a complaint, at the Southern Railway Company's annual meeting in Feb. 1935 [113], that the colour of the stock was too dowdy. Soon afterwards, an electric train on the Brighton line was recorded as being seen in a vivid green livery [114], but it was not until June 1938, after Bulleid's appointment, that production vehicles came out in this colour, and not until 1940 that it became general.

Colours

A:	Dark yellowish green	2·5 G 3/3 [96]
	Dark yellowish green	2·5 G 4/6 [49]
	Moderate green	5 G 5/6 [96]
	Dark green	7·5 G 3/6 [93]
	(Strong green	**7·5 G 4/7) [58]** ★ 7
	Dark bluish green	10 G 3/5 [94]
B:	Yellow [105]	
	Straw [102]	

One of the virtues claimed for this finish was that it would be long-wearing, and this certainly seems to have been true. The coach described in Appendix 2.10 for example, was apparently painted in the 1930s in olive green and only twice subsequently until it was withdrawn in 1966. The first coats of malachite green in the paint samples recently examined were still so resilient that they could be pared off with a knife without chipping. The intended life of the livery was ten years [105]. The livery was normally plain green without lining, but it had been intended to have two plain yellow lines below the windows as indicated in fig. 13s, and this decoration was applied to the stock built in 1938 for the second stage of the Portsmouth electrification scheme. The Company title was simplified to SOUTHERN, using 4 in. yellow and black transfers similar to those shown in figs. 6h and 9g. Besides new coaches, including the last three of the 1938 buffets, one G.P.O. van and some luggage vans were turned out with this form of lettering, and it also figured in an enlarged size on the driving ends of the post-war 4-SUB electric sets [115]. These originally had no cant-rail strip, so the upper limit of the green finish was the roof rain strip [105]. However, this marking was, on coaches as on locomotives, shortlived, and was replaced by the so-called "sunshine" lettering in approximately the same size as before, i.e. 4 in. It appears that the colours of these transfers were yellow and black only [35]. In the "pure" form of the livery,

Plate 1

a 2-2-2 no. 8 *Vesta* with tender no. 69 in the up platform road at Dorchester. Photo: Dorset County Museum collection, c. 1870.

b 2-4-0T no. 248. Location not identified, L & G R P 6014, n.d.

c Coat of arms transfer as used on locomotives 1895-1912, N. Pattenden's collection. Border divided in inches. Photo LRT 540-7, 12.68.

Plate 2

a 0-6-0ST no. 131 with two open wagons, apparently at Bournemouth Central. Wagon at right has Adams-type lettering, that at left has the later sort, apparently with a lessee's name on the top plank. Photo not identified, c. 1890.

b Unidentified A12 class 0-4-2 in Drummond passenger livery, with open wagons. Photo not identified, but endorsed "Exeter 1914". H. V. Tumilty's collection.

c **S11 class 4-4-0 no. 395 at Waterloo (unusually) before the 1911** rebuilding of the station, showing polished front end details, and arrangement of lining on cab front. Photo not identified.

Plate 3

a Ex-L B S C R D1 class 0-4-2T no. 2356 in full 1931 livery, showing numbers on rear panel. Photo Photomatic, c. 1934.

b O2 class 0-4-4T no. 192 with L B S C R type of numerals on the bunker. Photo not identified, c. 1935.

c "Battle of Britain" class 4-6-2 no. 21 C 168 *Kenley* at Cannon Street. Photo J. H. Aston, n.d.

Plate 4

a K10 class 4-4-0 no. 384 at Yeovil Town just before withdrawal. The engine is in black, but the tender is nominally green, and both 1942 and 1931 types of lettering are visible, as are the scar of the number plate on the rear panel and the lining. The tender was formerly that attached to no. 385 and the tops of those numbers can be seen on the side (cf the photo of the r.h. side given in Casserley, H. C., and Asher, L. L., *Locomotives of British Railways*, London, Spring Books, 1961, p. 206). Photo LRT, 1951.

b Carriage cleaners at Wimbledon posed in front of 3-car electric set no. E8 (car nos. 6712, 7558 and 7204). Lining and lettering are the later L S W R size and style. Photo, Museum of British Transport 365/11/64, 1915. Numbers from R. E. Tustin's records.

c Open wagon no. 9108 (steel underframe) being loaded in a rural yard. The right-hand wagon is of an earlier pattern. Photo not identified; (has been retouched before previous publication), c. 1910 judging by the oil-lubricated axleboxes.

Plate 5

a Basingstoke station, looking along the line of the present no. 4 platform. Photo not identified, Willis Museum p. 434, c. 1870.

b Basingstoke station after re-building, again looking along the line of the present no. 4 platform. Willis Museum p. 435, c. 1880.

Plate 6

a Alresford station looking north. Main building apparently painted dark brown (hence perhaps the white paint in the arches of the window reveals). Photo not identified; c. 1920 to judge by the girl's hat.

b The old station building at Christchurch, still in its L S W R colours of buff and dark brown with white window frames, a few years before its demolition in 1969. Photo LRT 443-7N, c. 3.1965.

c Iron level crossing gates in Spring Garden Lane, Gosport, just on the seaward side of the station, showing extemporised sheet-iron warning boards. Gate size 21 ft. 5½ in. hinge c.l. to stile, 4 ft. 3 in. centres of upper and lower rails. Photo LRT 537-8, 24.9.68.

Plate 7

a b
c
d

e

a Cast iron notice re Motor Car Acts 1896 and 1903 on bridge no. 13 in Cleveland Road, Bournemouth. Overall size 4 ft. 3 in. x 2 ft. 9 in. Photo LRT 545-2, 2.69.

b Enamelled sign at Petersfield station. Photo LRT 572-6. 11.1.70.

c Enamelled sign at Balham L T E station. Photo B. I. Fletcher V47-5, 1.3.69.

d Enamelled sign at Fratton goods office. Photo LRT 539-2, 5.10.68.

e Delivery cart (load 4t 0c 0q, tare 1t 8c 0q); faded letters S R on tilt and rear curtains. Photo, Museum of British Transport 39/66, n.d.

a

b c

Plate 8

a Delivery cart at Basingstoke during the rebuilding. Photo, Willis Museum P 438, Nov. 1903.

b Poster, 1930. Photo, Museum of British Transport 60/68.

c Poster, c. 1930. Photo, Museum of British Transport 73/68.

the title was placed as near the centre of the vehicle as was compatible with symmetry, and in line with the door handles if possible. Numbers were not moved but the class designations were marked in transferred figures on the lower parts of the door, as in fig. 13s, or on more modern stock (open thirds 1410-1450) alongside each door at eye level [35, 116]. These figures were similar to fig. 6k, but the coach number was often in less complicated figures like fig. 6g. In the conditions of the war, however it is not surprising that there were many variations of livery, especially on old stock. One common occurrence was to find a vehicle with an old paint finish bearing new transfers of the word SOUTHERN in the eaves panels; another was to find the coach number at both ends of each side. Blackout was maintained by painting the sides and bottom edges of the windows green (new stock only) — the guard's windows were completely painted over [105]. One simplifying factor was the temporary abolition of first class in the London area during the war. This led to the painting out of the door figures (fig. 13n [35]). When first class was reintroduced, rectangular transfers with those words were applied to the compartment windows — the precursor of present day B R practice.

The underframes and ends of coaches were not altered by the Bulleid changes, although the colour and style of set numbers were (compare figs. 13p and r) — later S R numbers are said to have been straw-coloured rather than yellow [102], (not white [117]). The end grab handles were painted yellow as was the cone end of the water tank filler pipe. The outside of the end door of the vestibule, and the fabric of the cover were black, as was the inclined handle of the guard's second door. The vestibule top cover was light tan leather [105].

3.18 Livestock vans.

These were originally painted as coaches, i.e. with white roof, green sides, and other parts black. Special cattle vans had the frames of drop and fixed lights grained teak, and the inside of the groom's compartment was stained oak with a white ceiling, while the cattle compartments were stone colour. The steam heater and its guard were purple brown [118]. The external lettering included a rather square S R, 12 in. high, but this was quickly altered to 4 in. Horseboxes were subject to the same scheme as the cattle vans [119].

A later scheme, probably a wartime measure [105], had the sides painted grey. The interior walls were buff, the floor black and the cushions red [120].

References

1. Exhibit in the Tudor House Museum, Southampton; the museum holds no evidence of its origin.
2. Hawkins, G., *The Holy Ghost Chapel and . . . the L S W R Station, Basingstoke, 1841,* Willis Museum, Basingstoke, ref. P431.
3. — , untitled, Guildford, 1842?, in Mr N. Pattenden's collection.
4. Anon. (probably Vallance, H. A.), *Railway Magazine*, v. 80, p. 141, (Feb. 1937). (Note from G. H. Platt).
5. Ellis, C. H., *The South Western Railway*, London, George Allen and Unwin, 1956, p. 36.
6. Ibid., p. 18.
7. Anon, *View from Chapel Hill*, Willis Museum, ref. P2525.
8. Ellis, C. H., *Railway Carriages in the British Isles from 1830 to 1914*, London, George Allen and Unwin, 1965, plate.
9. Williams, R. A., *The London and South Western Railway*, Newton Abbott, David and Charles, 1968, v. 1, p. 249, quoting the *Illustrated London News*. (This reference quotes extensive details of upholstery etc.)
10. Ellis, C. H., *The Trains we Loved*, London, George Allen and Unwin, 1955, p. 181.
11. Collinson, J., *Ordered on Foreign Service*, painting in the Museum of British Transport, Clapham, dated to 1862-70 by reference to the artist's productive period as given in Williamson, G.C. (ed.), *Bryan's Dictionary of Painters and Engravers*, London, G. Bell and Sons, 1913, v. 1, p. 316.
12. Smith, O. J., (1864-1930), recollections reported by his son.
13. Ellis, C. H., *British Railway History . . . , v. 1, 1830-1876*, London, George Allen and Unwin, 1954, coloured frontispiece.
14. Paint fragments described in Appendix 2.2.
15. Ellis, *SWR*, p. 97.
16. Ellis, *SWR*, p. 98.
17. Slinn, J. N., *HMRS Livery Register no. 2, Great Western Railway*, Reading, Historical Model Railway Society, 1967, p. 12.
18. Ellis, *RCBI*, p. 119.
19. Ellis, C. H., *Nineteenth Century Railway Carriages . . . ,* London, Modern Transport Publishing Co., 1949, p. 52.
20. L S W R drawing no. 2478 dated 17th June 1879: 30 ft. second-class six-wheel coach.
21. L S W R drawing no. 2260 dated 23rd Jan. 1877: 24 ft. 6 in. 1st/2nd class composite coach.

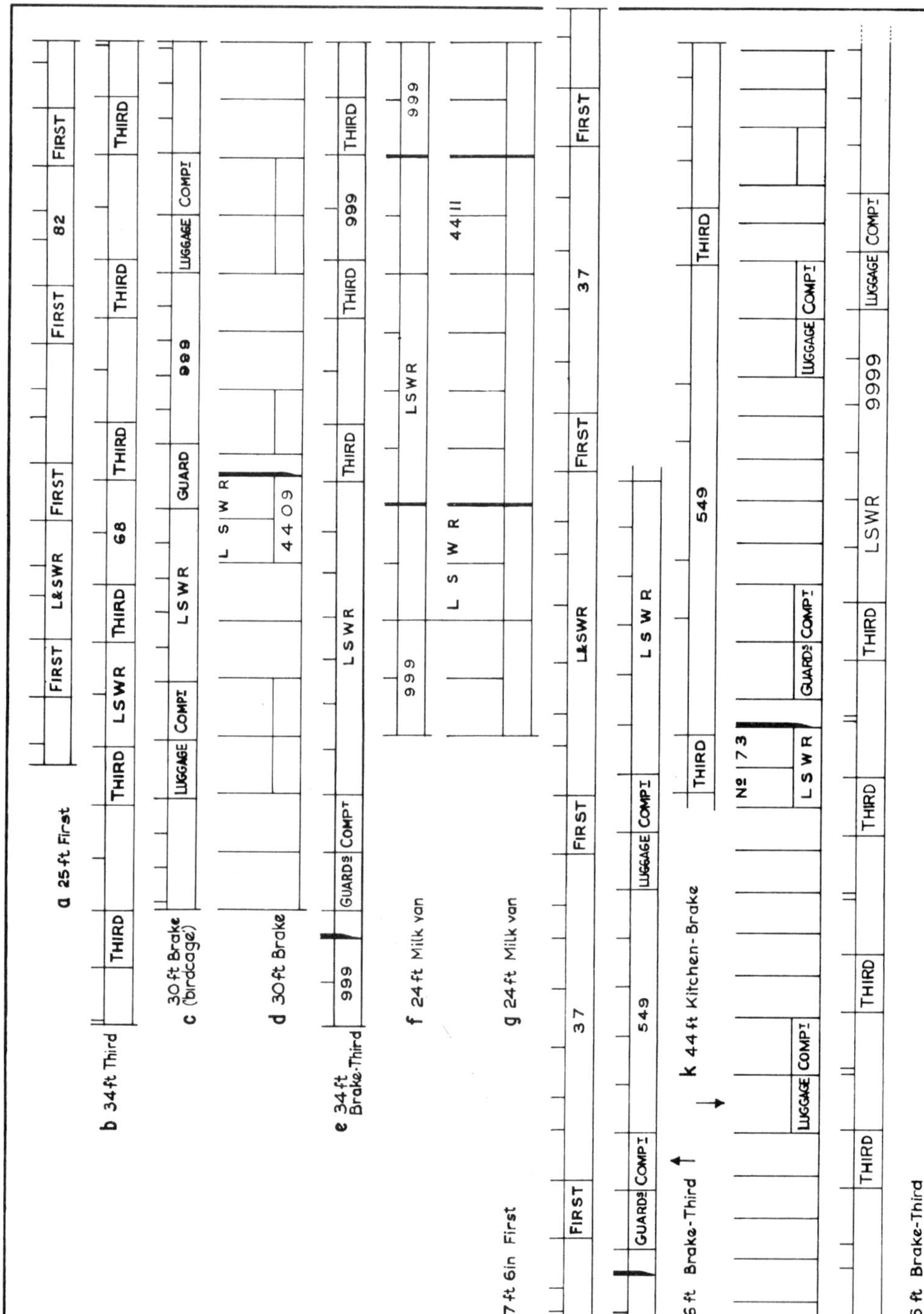

Fig. 12 Layout of L S W R coach lettering

not to scale

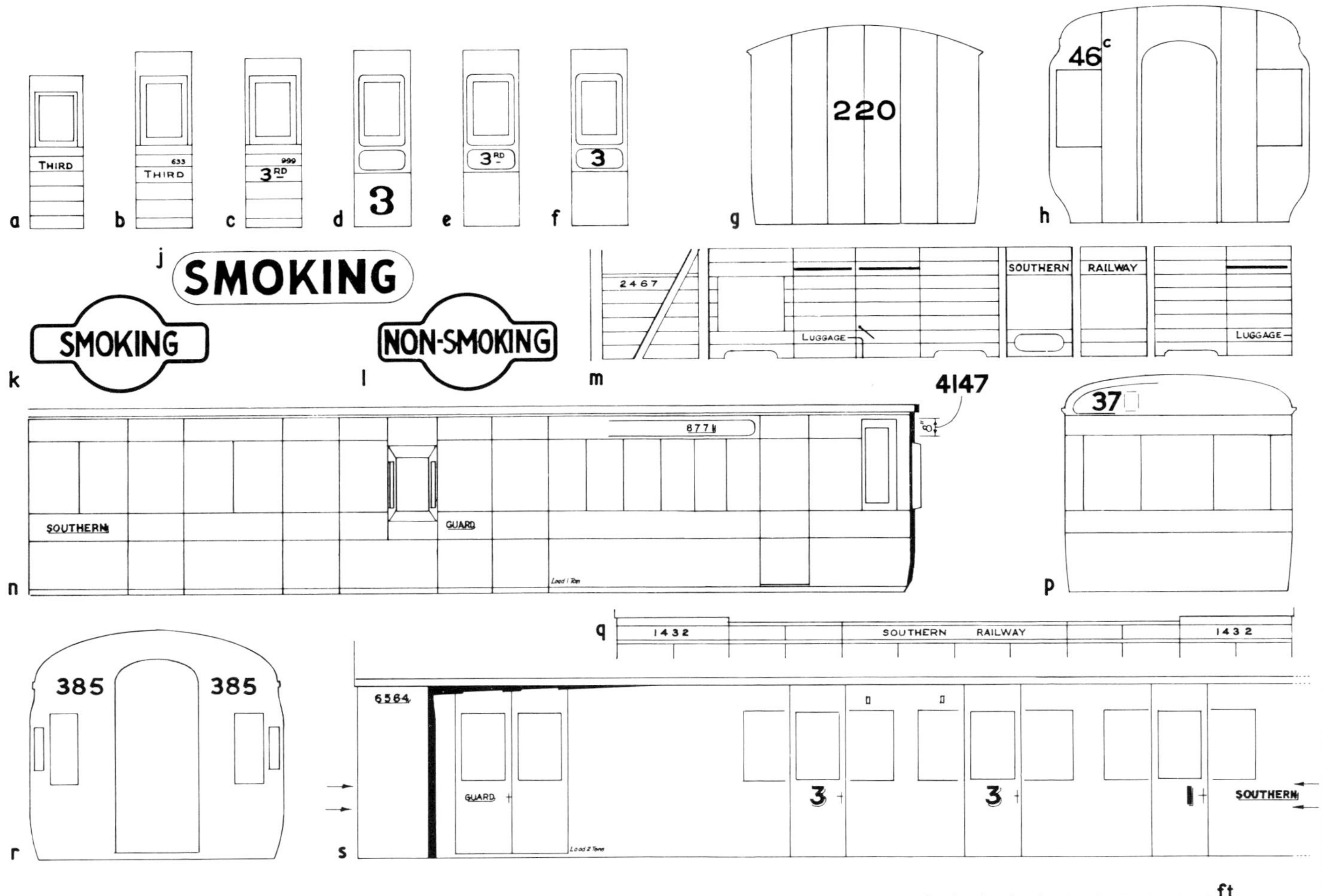

Fig. 13 Layout of LSWR and SR coach lettering

22. Ellis, C. H., *Four Main Lines*, London, George Allen and Unwin, 1950, p. 199.
23. Ellis, *S W R*, p. 128.
24. Bushell, A. M., *Railway Magazine*, v. 63, p. 408 (Nov. 1928).
25. BTHR LSW 1/186, entry nos. 208, 296.
26. *South Western Gazette*, no. 56 (1st Nov. 1885).
27. BTHR LSW 5/11.
28. Paint fragments described in Appendix 2.3.
29. Paint fragments described in Appendix 2.4.
30. Paint fragments described in Appendix 2.5.
31. Paint fragments described in Appendix 2.1.
32. From study of photographs, particularly that of 43 ft. first-class coach no. 175 (1892) reproduced in Marshall, C. F. D. (revised by R. W. Kidner), *History of the Southern Railway, v. 1*, London, Ian Allan, 1963, f.p. 104.
33. BTHR LSW 1/186, entry no. 1138.
34. Ibid., entry no. 1311.
35. From study of photographs.
36. Measured details obtained from body of 19 ft. 11 in. third-class coach grounded at Bournemouth West (see also Appendix 2.2).
37. Measured details obtained from coach door of c. 1870 in the Museum of British Transport. The door is greatly discoloured.
38. Tumilty, H. V., measured details obtained from body of 30 ft. second-class coach grounded at St. Kew Highway (see also Appendix 2.3).
39. Inferred from photograph in Marshall, op. cit., f.p. 32.
40. Tumilty, H. V., from study of photographs.
41. *Railway Engineer*, v. 21, p. 172 (June 1900).
42. The writer has to retract his first opinion of Mr Peacock's version of "salmon". It was in fact rather more red than any surviving sample, but so much nearer than any imitation produced for modelling purposes (except Mr. F. W. Bush's) that it gave grounds for believing that Nine Elms paint shops did at least *take notice* of the recipes which have come down to us.
43. Knight, D. W., private communication.
44. Gundry, G. L., *South Western Circular*, no. 15, pp. 107-8 (1968).
45. Nock, O.S., *The London and South Western Railway*, London, Ian Allan, n.d. but 1965, p. 98.
46. Tustin, R. E., *Model Railway News*, v. 29, p. 188 (Sept. 1953).
47. Collins, J. B. B., *Railway Magazine*, v. 15, p. 287 (Nov. 1904).
48. Ellis, *SWR*, p. 19.
49. Paint fragments described in Appendix 2.6.
50. S R drawing no. E 4036 amend. 1 dated 16th Dec. 1936: Painting diagram of 49 ft. bogie passenger brake van in old L S W R colours, quoted by Mr. A. F. J. Kerr in private communication.
51. Ellis, C. H., *The Beauty of Old Trains*, London, George Allen and Unwin 1952, coloured frontispiece.
52. Peacock, C. J., colour value obtained from contemporary model of compartment of an L S W R coach, exhibit no. 1264/52 in the Museum of British Transport (private communication).
53. Sample panel produced in August 1948 by B R workshops using paints reconstituted from the formulae given in Appendices 1.6 and 1.9; circumstances stated in letter from A. B. MacLeod to J. N. Maskelyne, 25th Aug. 1948.
54. Maskelyne, J. N., *Model Railway News*, v. 24, p. 203 (Nov. 1948).
55. Barnes, P. E., *South Western Circular*, no. 15, p. 110 (1968), his contemporary description.
56. Ibid., recording a comment by an L S W R employee. How apt this is can be appreciated by anyone who tries to establish the colour of the 10 ft. 0 in. second-class and 14 ft. 10 in. third-class Bodmin and Wadebridge coaches in the Railway Museum, York, which are apparently the last surviving vehicles with a complete L S W R-applied paint scheme.
57. The writer, colour from model compartment (see note 53).
58. Howard Turner, J. T., colours from his contemporary models; and recollections in text.
59. Ellis, *SWR*, colour plate f.p. 64.
60. Stevens, C., contemporary phrase recollected in private communication with C. J. Peacock.
61. Ellis, *BOT*, p. 15.
62. Carter, E. F., *Britain's Railway Liveries . . . 1825-1948*, London, Harold Starke, 1963, colour chart.
63. Tustin, R. E., *Model Railway News*, v. 26, p. 128 (July 1950).
64. Ellis, *SWR*, p. 20.
65. Warner, Surrey, in Macaulay, J. (ed.), *Modern Railway Working*, London, Gresham Publishing Co., 1912, v. 5, 149.
66. Exposed paint on body of 24 ft. parcels van at Twyford, Berks., Sept. 1967.
67. Tumilty, H. V., noted from grounded body described in Appendix 2.3.
68. Photograph in *Locomotive Magazine*.
69. Warner, Surrey, quoted in Howden, J. R., *Boys' Book of Railways*, 1909.
70. Photograph in *Railway Magazine*, v. 2, pp. 318 ff (April 1898).
71. Tumilty, H. V., notes from drawings and contemporary published descriptions, including *Railway* Magazine, v. 14, p. 353 (May 1904).
72. Exhibit in the Museum of British Transport.

73. Burtt, F., *L S W R Locomotives, a Survey 1872-1923,* London, Ian Allan, n.d. but c. 1950 p. 63.
74. Bradley, D. L., *Locomotives of the London and South Western Railway*, Lichfield, Staffs., Railway Correspondence and Travel Society, pt. 2, 1967, p. 86.
75. Chorley, R., *Model Railway Constructor*, v. 35, pp. 247-9 (Aug. 1968). The colours named in this article do not agree with samples; but Mr. Chorley informs me that they were named on the basis of a verbal account.
76. Burtt, op. cit., p. 74.
77. Bradley, op. cit., p. 118.
78. Ibid., p. 120.
79. Warner, S., in Bell, A. R. et al (eds.), *Railway Mechanical Engineering,* London, Gresham Publishing Co., 1923, v. 1, p. 169.
80. Ellis, *SWR*, p. 198.
81. Tustin, R. E., *Model Railway News*, v. 28, p. 95 (May 1952).
82. BTHR LSW 1/12.
83. Moody, G. T., *Southern Electric 1909-1968*, London, Ian Allan, 1968, p. 16.
84. It is questioned that the official name for this colour was that current in connexion with locomotives.
85. Nock, op. cit., p. 147.
86. Ellis, *SWR*, p. 215.
87. Paint fragments described in Appendix 2.7.
88. Tustin, R. E., *Model Railway News*, v. 26, p. 10 (Jan. 1950).
89. Tustin, R. E., private communication.
90. Warner, S., in Bell, op. cit., p. 182.
91. Ibid., p. 181.
92. Paint fragment N367-2 from ex-S E C R coach used as a store at Exeter.
93. Paint fragments described in Appendix 2.8.
94. Paint fragments described in Appendix 2.9.
95. Paint specimen supplied from Ashford works in 1929 to Mr. S. B. Dent.
96. Paint fragments described in Appendix 2.10.
97. Paint fragment N367-3 from unidentified coach in Departmental use at Wimbledon.
98. S R drawing no. E 14252 dated 1925: Lining for steel panelled stock.
99. Dent, S. B., private communication of recollections.
100. S R, *Eastleigh Locomotive Works* (booklet published for public tours), probably first published before 1933.
101. See Slinn, op. cit., p. 37.
102. Williams, A., private communication.
103. S R drawing no. 14015, Lining on 8 ft. 6 in. wide electric stock.
104. S R drawing no. 14185, Lining on South-Western section 9 ft. wide stock.
105. Chorley, R., private communication.
106. Tustin, R. E., measured details obtained from panel of an ex-Lynton and Barnstaple Rly. coach in his collection.
107. Measured details from body of 24 ft. milk van grounded at Wickham (see also Appendix 2.7).
108. Foote, F., *Model Railway News,* v. 27, pp. 180-1 (Sept. 1951).
109. Tustin, R. E., *Model Railway News*, v. 27, p. 216 (Nov. 1951).
110. Probably referred to in *Railway Magazine*, v. 76, p. 60 (Jan. 1935).
111. Bishop, M., measured details from window of an ex-Lynton and Barnstaple Rly. coach in his collection.
112. Bishop, M. private communication.
113. *Railway Magazine*, v. 76, p. 295 (Apr. 1935).
114. *Railway Magazine*, v. 78, p. 232 (Mar. 1936).
115. Kichenside, G. M., *Railway Carriage Album*, London, Ian Allan, 1966, p. 195.
116. Moody, op. cit., photos, pp. 32(c), 49(a).
117. Stevens-Stratton, S. W., *Model Railway Constructor*, v. 34, p. 350 (Nov. 1967) .
118. S R drawing nos. E 19144 and E 19145, Feb. 1930.
119. S R drawing no. E 19519.
120. S R drawing no. 27213, Aug. 1936.

4.1 Up to 1885.

The earliest livery which is known to have been applied to L S W R wagons is that current from c. 1895 onward; this was plain brown (see Section 4.3). Photographs from the period of Adams' term of office generally show a dark colour (again probably brown) with small lettering L & S W R. But there are a few pieces of evidence for an earlier livery. One is a photograph [1] of a single-plank wagon (fig. 15b) with the letters L & S W R CO in the centre of the side with the number 1882 underneath. Another photograph [2] shows a four-plank wagon with the same initials on the second plank to the left centre of the drop flap (fig. 15a). A contemporary painting [3] shows open wagons of an early L S W R end profile [4] painted medium grey. The painting appears to be reliable on points of detail [5] and probably dates from c. 1880. It is suggested that a livery combining these features may have been in use in the later Beattie period.

4.2 The Adams period.

A paint described as "zinc brown" was tried out early in 1887, and authorised to be kept in stock on 19th January of that year [6]. This may indicate the date of the changeover from the earlier livery postulated above.

The usual lettering was L & S W R to the left, and the wagon number to the right of the drop flap (fig. 15c [7]). All the photographs showing this arrangement seem to date from after Adams' arrival as Mechanical Engineer and it is possible that he introduced this style of lettering, as it followed closely that used by the Great Eastern Railway from its earliest years [8]. However, vans (including brake vans) with sliding doors had the letters grouped above the number (fig. 15d [9]). It seems likely that brake vans had red ends as in later years, but no direct evidence of this has come to light.

4.3 The later L S W R period.

Under W. Panter, who was responsible for L S W R carriages and wagons from 1885 to 1905, the foregoing livery appears to have been continued, but large company initials were introduced at some time previous to 1900 [10]. They had a distinctly North-Western appearance and this was not the only resemblance between the rolling stock of the two companies. Combined with a rearrangement of numbering and smaller lettering, which was now as shown in figs. 16 a-d, j, k, m, n [11], this scheme lasted until the grouping.

Colours:

A: Wagon brown [12]
Dark brown [13, 14, 15]
Dark brown . . . weathering to a terra cotta shade [16]
Dark umber brown with black underframes and white letters [17]
Very dark umber [18]
Dark brown, no. 3-039 of BS 2660: 1955 5 YR 1·5/4 [19] ★ 15
Dark grayish yellowish brown, no. 3-038 of BS 2660: 1955 10 YR 3/2 [20]
(Dark grayish brown 5 YR 1·5/2 est.) [21]

B: Dull red (probably red oxide) [21]

C: *Lead* [14]
Dark bluish gray, no. 632 of BS 381C: 1964 10 B 4/0·5 [?]

The approved method of painting wagons was as follows [14]. Steel underframes pickled in a solution of sulphuric acid and water for about half an hour. Taken out and well drained, then placed in an alkaline solution of lime water for a quarter of an hour to kill acid, and afterwards dipped in clean water. When dry, members painted with two coats of graphite paint.

Wood underframes and bodies one coat of lead colour, followed by puttying up where required and a further coat of lead colour. When thoroughly dry both body and outside of underframe should have one coat of dark brown. The required lettering and numbering to be done in white, all ironwork, buffers, axleboxes etc. to be blacked up. The inside of body to receive one coat of lead colour.

This was the specification current in c. 1912; after the war the finicky work of painting the small ironwork was not usually done [23]. Surrey Warner seems to have intended the interval between paintings to be about four years [24], but in fact many wagons were not repainted and renumbered by the S R until 1930, and although the process was substantially complete as regards L S W R stock by that year, some wagons carried their pre-grouping identities until as late as 1936 [23]. The ends of brake vans were painted dull red [21], probably in the fashion later adopted by the S R (see Section 4.7); it seems likely that headstocks and buffer guides were also red [25]. Roofs and wheel tyres were white ex factory [11], and the lettering consisted of the company initials, nominally 12 in. high [11], but varying in practice from 11½ in. [26] to 13 in. [27], and reduced to 8 in. on short bolster wagons [28] and also on some goods brake vans [29]. The form of the letters was normally as shown in fig. 14c, but they were hand-painted (not, apparently, stencilled) and so irregularities were sometimes to be seen [11]. No prominent initials were carried by "aero" wagons because they had been cheaply converted from 28 ft. road van carriers by the removal of the side planks [30]. Wagon numbers were painted at the right-hand end of each side, usually in six-inch figures [11, 26, 27], but five inches high on bolster wagons [28], and generally just below the Company initials on open wagons (figs. 16b, c [11]). However, from about 1910 they were moved down to the lowest plank, probably to enable them to be read under a tarpaulin [27, 31]. The numbers of hinged-door vans were marked high up on the side, and goods brakes were similarly treated (figs. 16d, n [11]), while cattle trucks had the number on the top plank at the right-hand of each side, and also at the same level in the left-hand panel of each end, probably in case the number on the side became obscured by whitewash, which as usual was freely applied to the interior of the truck and washed out through every aperture (fig. 16p [11]). Tare weights and capacities were marked in plain and italic letters, along the lower edge of the body, using a basic size of two inches high, with three-inch capitals (figs. 14e, f [11, 27]). Standard wagon number plates are shown in figs. 17a, c. [32]; these appear to have been painted brown [33] with white lettering [11]. The name of the home station of brake vans, when shown, appeared in the bottom right-hand corner of the body side, in about 5 in. lettering [34].

4.4 Refrigerator vans

These were the one main exception to the general brown livery, as they were painted a light colour to reduce heat intake. The earliest date established for this livery is 1907 [35], and the basic colour is, in common with the other L S W R shades of pink or stone, a matter of some dispute [36].

Colours:

A: Salmon [15, 18]
  Shrimp pink . . . might have been some form of stone [37]
  Light stone [38]
  Yellowish white, no. 4-064 of BS 2660: 1955 — 5 Y 9·25/1 [39]
  (Moderate pink — **10 RP 7/4 est.)** [21]

B: **Crimson** [21]
  Venetian red [38]
  (n.b. this colour was probably the same as S R colour B of Section 4.7)

C: Either black or a dirty yellow [37]

The basic colour was applied both to the body and to the solebars [11, 37], but some vans had dark solebars although whether black or dark brown is not known [37]. Possibly the dark solebars were those with iron flitch-plates, which would be expected to be black as on ordinary wagons with steel underframes. But ironwork was not in general painted black. The lettering L S W R was red [21], but other lettering seems to have been black (although later white [34]), and it is possible that the Company initials were themselves black to begin with [37, 38]. This livery seems to have been introduced before 1907, but refrigerator vans were for some years after their introduction painted in what appeared to be the standard brown livery [11].

4.5 Wagons acquired from the S & D J R in 1914 retained their gray livery, only being re-marked with L S W R lettering and having an L S W R number plate fitted [40].

4.6. Tarpaulins were black with white letters [41], usually of the form shown on fig. 18a [11], but it is possible that block letters were used after the war, although this is not certain because it is difficult to be sure if a sheet is a wagon type or one for use on a road vehicle. Carter gives two alternate forms of the Company initials, viz.: L S W R and L & S W R [42].

4.7 Southern Railway wagons.

The goods stock livery adopted by the S R was more than superficially related to that of the L S W R, but there were apparently three distinguishable varieties of the basic brown colour, one of which, A1, was, to judge from surviving samples, nearly the same as the L S W R goods brown, while a second was notionally the old L B S C R coach colour and perhaps only used at the Central section works before about 1930. A3 seems to have been the result of prolonged weathering of A1.

Colours:

A1: *Standard brown* [43] — Appendix 1.17
  Dark brown, no. 3-039 of BS 2660:1955 — **5 YR 1·5/4** [44] ★ 15
  weathering to
  Brownish gray — 10 YR 3/1 [44]
  Brownish gray — 10 YR 3/0·5 [45]
  Dark grayish yellowish brown, no. 3-038 of BS 2660: 1955 — 10 YR 3/2 [22]

A2: *Coach umber* — Appendix 1·16
  Dark reddish brown — 10 R 3/4 [46]

A3: Dark orange yellow, no. 359 of BS 381C: 1964 — 10 YR 6·5/8 [47]

B: *Venetian red* [48, 49]
  This colour definitely *appeared* vermilion [50]
  Vivid red, no. 1-024 of BS 2660: 1955 — 7·5 R 3/12 [20]
  weathering to
  Strong reddish brown, no. 447 of BS 381C: 1964 — **10 R 3/8** [20] ★ 16
  (Moderate reddish orange, no. 1-023 of BS 2660: 1955 — 7·5 R 5/8 [51])

C: Dark gray [52]

D: Purple brown, the former L S W R locomotive colour (see Section 2.9) [53]

As before, the general colour was dark brown, and this colour seems to have been used for the solebars and headstocks also, as a black patch was called for, on which could be chalked the oiling dates [43]. It seems likely that fittings below the solebars were also brown. Mr. West has recorded [52] one ex-LSWR open wagon, no. 4058E, in dark grey (1939) and this may not have been an isolated case. The ends of goods brake vans were painted Venetian red [48, 49] (which seems to have taken on a wide range of tints) and while the drawings are silent upon the point [43], the headstocks were also painted this colour, even, for a while, on the short-cabined "pillbox" type of van introduced by the S R [34], although the early photographs of the type seem to show that the fittings on the headstocks were black [48]. The interior colouring of brake vans was purple brown up to the waist line (actually 3 ft. 2 in. above the floor), with stone colour (see Section 4.8) above a 1½ in. black dividing line [53]. The interiors of verandahs were painted dark brown, except that the windowed partition was painted Venetian red down to the level of the tops of the side doors; the ceiling was white [48], as were the exterior commode handles [43].

S R lettering differed from that of the L S W R in that the smaller writing was entirely in block letters, and also conformed to (or pioneered) the practice of the other grouped companies in having the wagon number at the left end of the side (figs. 14h, j, k [11, 43], 16g [11]). The Company initials were of the form shown in fig. 14g [55]; the official drawings did not specify the exact form, but only the dimensions [43]. Miscellaneous writing on the solebars is shown in fig. 16r [43].

4.8 Insulated and ventilated vans.

These had a light-coloured finish as they had in L S W R days.

Colour:

Light stone, no. 61 of BS 381C: 1930 [43] (n.b., this colour was revised to a cleaner appearance and redesignated as Light Stone, no. 361 of BS 381C: 1948, and subsequently Light Stone, no. 361 of BS 381C: 1964 1 Y 6·5/5)

Moderate yellowish pink 2·5 YR 8/5 [21] ★ 17 discolouring to

Light yellowish brown, no. 3-043 of BS 2660: 1955 10 YR 6·5/5 [21]

It may be noted that the shade of this colour was apparently, before weathering, within the range of colours established for L S W R coach "salmon" (see Section 3.10 and Appendix 3), and this suggests that there was a continuity between the L S W R and S R schemes, although the paint sample [21] and Mr. Werrett's drawing [40] show that the S R stone colouring was applied to L S W R vans which had been brown, as well as to the older refrigerator vans. The main colour was applied to the sides, ends and headstocks, while the solebars were painted standard brown [43, 54, 55] and buffers and ironwork below the solebars, black [11]. The smaller lettering as well as the Company initials, was red (colour B of Section 4.7) [56], but in a few cases the N indicating "non-common user" was painted white [57]. A less-pink type of stone, agreeing with the building colour (B of Section 6.7, ★ 18) seems to have been used also [58].

4.9 Refrigerator vans.

Ex-L S W R vans were painted in the stone livery described above [56], but S R-built vans were white with black underframes and lettering [59].

4.10 Standardisation of identification.

The Southern Railway adopted the practice of concentrating the Company initials, capacity and wagon number in the bottom left corner of the side (figs. 16f [55], h [43]) or low down on a sliding door (fig. 16q [44]) from 1936 onwards [43]. The sizes of the markings were approximately constant and are shown in fig. 15.1-p [43, 44]. The normal colouring was white [11], but on stone-coloured vans red was used [55] and on white vans, black [59]. Wagon number plates were of several forms; ex-L S W R wagons just had the plate turned round to face the solebar, and the S R number, with a suffix E, painted on the back. S R-built wagons had rather smaller elliptical plates (fig. 17b [60]), although wagons with R.C.H.. underframes had segmental plates from 1927 at least (fig. 17d [61]).

4.11. Wartime changes.

The most general change was the decision in 1942 to reduce the painting of wagons to a minimum. From this date, open wagons at least were to have their metal parts painted black, and their planking left unpainted except for the bottom left corner planks, which were to be painted black as a background for white lettering comprising N (3 in.), OOT (2 in.), S R 9999 (3 in.) and, in the bottom right corner of the side, the tare weight 9-99 [43]:

A curious change was made in the livery of meat and banana vans in April/March 1941 respectively. Their former light colouring was replaced [43] by:

Colours:

A: *Red oxide,* no. 46 of BS 381C: 1930

B: *Lemon,* no. 55 of BS 381C: 1930

Earlier changes on meat vans were the alteration of the code word MEVA to MEAT, which was marked in 4 in. letters and amplified by FOR FRESH MEAT in 2½ in. letters. At the same time the non-pool letters N were deleted. This was in Dec. 1940 [43], and in the next month the colour of the lettering was altered to black [43]. When the main colouring was altered in April, the solebars remainder brown [43]. The banana vans had their lettering RETURN TO S'TON DOCKS deleted in December 1940 also [43]; the van shown in fig. 16f was apparently lettered BOULOGNE [44]. Possibly in 1941, banana vans had green bands added to all four corners as indicated isometrically on the meat van drawing, fig. 16r [43]. The wartime changes were probably intended to reduce the conspicuousness of the vans for two reasons: (i) to avoid drawing attention to which ports were handling perishable imports, and (ii) to reduce slightly the risk of pilfering of black-marketable goods. The green markings on banana vans, if they were indeed intended to signify the vans' contents in a discreet manner, also presumably indicate that the banana traffic did continue on however reduced a scale.

With similar discretion, gunpowder vans had their inscription deleted and replaced by a black 5 in. dia. disc with a ½ in. wide white outline and a 3 in. letter C in the centre. This change applied only from 1940 to 1945 [43]. The non-pool Ns were also affected; the right-hand ones only were deleted around 1940 [43].

4.12 Containers.

This subject is not well studied, and a large number of types existed. There seem to have been even more liveries than container types.

Colours:

A: *Stone* (see Section 4.8) [43].

B: *Venetian Red* (colour B of Section 4.7) [43]

C: *Standard brown* (colour A1 of Section 4.7) [43]

D: *Sea green, no. 17 of BS 381C:1930* [62] no. 6-066 of BS 2660: 1955 2·5 G 6/2 [21]

E: *Red oxide,* (colour A of Section 4.11) [43]

F: *Yellow* (colour B of Section 4.11) [43]

G: *Standard green* (colour A2 of Section 3.16) [62]

H: *Orange, no. 57 of BS 381C:1930* [62] Yellow [21, 63]

J: *Portland stone, no. 64 of BS 381C:1930* [62]

Table 1

type	fig.	cap. tons	tare t c q	dimensions internal l x w x h	dimensions external l x w x h	doors	livery note	source of information
Insulated	19a	3½	1 1 2		12′0″x7′0″x6′3″ est	S E	1	S R photograph
Insul meat F	19b	3½	1 9 2		12′0″x6′1″x6′11″(side)	S E	2	E.B. Trotter
Insulated		3½		12′0″x5′7½″x6′6″				S R booklet
Insulated	19d	3½			13′4″x x6′2″ est.	S E	1	" "
(road service)								
Insulated F	19e				14′8″x x7′0″ est.	S E	4	photograph
Ventilated M	19f	3	2 9 0		15′6″x x7′4″ est.	S E?	5	S R booklet
Ventilated		4		15′6½″x6′8½″x7′3″				" "
Furniture K	19g	4	1 10 3		15′3″x7′0″x6′8″(side)	E	6	" " and dim'ns per E.B. Trotter
Furniture	19h	4		15′0″x6′9″x7′0″		E	6	" " and notes by R. Chorley
?		4	1 10 2 (av.)		16′0″x7′0″x7′11½″ (9′0″ slats on roof)	E		S R Diagram
? A?	19c	4	1 - -		14′0″x7′0″x6′2″ est.	S E	3	S R booklet
Large		4		13′8¾″x6′4¾″x6′6″				" "
Small		2½		7′0″x6′7¼″x6′8″				" "
Small		3			7′6″x7′0″x7′11⅝″			S R Diagram
Small open		2½ or 4		6′11½″x5′11½″x3′0″				S R booklet
Large open		3		12′0″x6′0″x3′6″				

Table 1 gives a summary of known dimensions and liveries, and is illustrated by fig. 19.

1. The containers used for meat traffic were painted as for meat vans in the manner shown in fig. 19a [11]. The official drawing, no. E 17514, shows the container number raised to 6 in. under the S [43]. Fig. 19d shows a similar livery in stone and Venetian red [64].
2. A livery corresponding with the 1936 revision of wagon lettering is shown in fig. 19b. The colours are stone with black letters [63].
3. Apparently an early example of a general-purpose container, that shown in fig. 19c had a livery of C with white letters [43, 64].
4. A later practice, c. 1934, was to build containers in aluminium, which was not painted [21]. Before the war the type shown in fig. 19e was lettered in G, but with S R in colour B [43], although they were alternatively lettered in D [21].
5. Ventilated containers were aluminium with letters in D [65]. During the war, a livery of E with letters in F was adopted (cf. Section 4.11) [43].
6. Furniture containers had elaborate liveries for advertisement. The basic colour was D, while the lesser lettering and Company initials were colour G, as were the zig-zag motifs [21, 63]. The slogan on these panels has been noted in yellow [21, 63], although the drawings called for colour J with a ⅛ in. outline in colour H [62]. A ¼ in. band of H also surrounded the motifs [62], and the position of the end lettering is shown as on a photo [66] although the drawings showed it lower [62]. Containers of this type were nos. K 590-629 and BK 791-815 [43]. The wartime livery for furniture containers is shown in fig. 19h [67].

4.13 Tarpaulins. Fig. 18b shows S R tarpaulin lettering of c. 1925 [11].

References

1. In *Railway Magazine,* v. 74, p. 266 (April 1934), showing the Stephen Lewin engine *Cheshire,* built 1875, apparently being delivered on this wagon.
2. Of L S W R no. 151 *Montrose* as rebuilt in 1891.
3. In the Tudor House Museum, Southampton.
4. Cf. photographs in Bradley, D. L., *Locomotives of the London and South Western Railway,* Solihull, Railway Correspondence and Travel Society, pt. 1, 1965, figs. 46, 71.
5. Tavender, L., in *HMRS Journal,* v. 6, pp. 148-50 (1969).
6. BTHR LSW 1/186, entry no. 822.
7. From a photograph of 0–6–0ST no. 131 (plate 2a).
8. Information on the dating of the G E R style from Mr J. Watling.
9. From a photograph of Swanage station (opened 1885) in Ellis, C. H., *The South Western Railway,* London, George Allen and Unwin, 1956, f.p. 81.
10. Date established from photographs of goods brake vans nos. 10131 and 11104, which were built in 1895/7 and had large initials before they were fitted with side lights in 1901 onwards.
11. From photographs.
12. BR–SR under reference "per C & W Engineer, Eastleigh, CW 90/27, C/Y 7.9.55".
13. Collins, J. B. B., in *Railway Magazine,* v. 15, p. 285 (Nov. 1904).
14. Warner, S., in Macaulay, J. (ed.), *Modern Railway Working,* London, Gresham Publishing Co., 1912, v. 5, p. 151.
15. Ellis, C. H., *The Trains We Loved,* London, George Allen and Unwin, 1955, p. 181.
16. Carter, E. F., *Britain's Railway Liveries . . . 1825-1948,* London, Harold Starke, 1963, p. 136.
17. *Moore's Monthly Magazine,* v. 1, p. 36 (May 1896), quoted in *HMRS Journal,* v. 3, p. 88 (1961).
18. Ellis, *SWR, p.* 198.
19. Knight, D. W., private communication, colour identified by recollections of his relatives.
20. Paint fragment described in Appendix 2.11.
21. Howard Turner, J. T., private communication, colour from his contemporary models.
22. Paint fragment described in Appendix 2.12.
23. Hemingway, G. Y., private communication of contemporary observations.
24. Warner, S., in Bell, A. R. et al. (eds.), *Railway Mechanical Engineering,* London, Gresham Publishing Co., 1923, v. 1, p. 182.

25. Tumilty, H. V., private communication, result of study of photographs.
26. Hemingway, G. Y., HMRS drawing no. 16 W 494, 12 ton 31 ft. 0 in. drop-side wagon no. 9323.
27. Hemingway, drawing no. 16 W 491, 10 ton 15 ft. 4 in. open wagon no. 1532.
28. Hemingway, drawing no. 16 W 497, 10 ton 13 ft. 1 in. bolster wagon no. 1859.
29. Photograph of brake van no. 44 in *HMRS Journal,* v. 6, p. 64 (1968).
30. Hemingway, drawing no. 16 W 493, 10 ton 28 ft. 0 in. flat wagon no. 13569.
31. This may not have been a general practice, as few pictures show it.
32. Measured details from a plate in the collection of Mr M. Palmer.
33. Tumilty, H. V., private communication after examining the plate from wagon no. 7706, in his collection.
34. Howard Turner, J. T., private communication of recollections.
35. Tumilty, H. V., from consideration of the building date of the earliest wagons known to have been painted in this livery.
36. But the intention of the L S W R to use a colour like that in use on buildings does not seem to be in doubt.
37. Stevens, C., private communication of recollections from c. 1904 (n.b.) to C. J. Peacock.
38. Edwards Bros., drawing no. 17/17.
39. Pattenden, N., private communication of colour identified by a relative.
40. Werrett, K. A., drawing in *Model Railway News,* v. 40, p. 415 (July 1964).
41. Tumilty, H. V., private communication quoting former worker in Nine Elms sheet shop.
42. Carter, op. cit., p. 345.
43. Chorley, R., private communication quoting S R drawings.
44. Paint fragment no. N 367–8 and measured details both from S R van no. 42099 (ex L S W R no. 8501), grounded at Lower Upham, Hants.
45. Paint fragment no. 367-4 from unidentified S R wagon.
46. Exposed paint on body of unidentified ex-L S W R van grounded at Bishop's Waltham, Hants.
47. Recollection by the writer of colour of ex-L B S C R van no. 3605, c. 1951.
48. Sparkes, Maj. -, ("Sparks"), in *Model Railway News,* v. 5, p. 340 (Nov. 1929).
49. S R drawings, no. E 4091 dated 1924, and no. L/E 4738.
50. Blackburn, A., private communication of recollection.
51. Colour value obtained from "Kodachrome II" transparency of ex-S R van no. 55677, taken in 1963.
52. West, A. E., in *South Western Circular,* no. 1 (Autumn 1964).
53. Chorley, R., in *Model Railway Constructor,* v. 32, p. 238 (Sept. 1965).
54. Trotter, E. B., in *Model Railway Constructor,* v. 31, p. 158 (June 1964) gives black underframes, but this would have rendered the black oiling-date patch superfluous.
55. Noted from grounded body described in Appendix 2.11.
56. Tumilty, H. V., private communication of notes from body of van no. 50018 (ex L S W R no. 12389 of 1899) grounded at Camelford.
57. Blackburn, A., in *Model Railway Constructor,* v. 33, p. 237 (Sept. 1966).
58. Meccano Ltd., Hornby-Dublo model of S R meat van no. 51298; 1936 livery.
59. Blackburn, A., in *Model Railway Constructor,* v. 33, p. 108 (Apr. 1966).
60. From a plate in Mr D. J. Wigley's collection (S R utility van).
61. From a plate in Mr R. E. Gilbert's collection.
62. S R drawing no. E 23075.
63. Trotter, E. B., private communication of details from bodies.
64. Southern Railway, *Distribution Services* (pamphlet), n.d. but c. 1930, p. 16.
65. Ibid., p. 26 and S R photo no. M 153 of 1934.
66. *Distribution Services,* p. 13
67. S R photo no. M 513, 1943.

Section 5 Departmental stock

5.1 L S W R Engineer's Department locomotives

Up to 1883 at least, engines used for ballast trains were painted green [1, 2]. The shade was a bright green "similar to that of the present L N E R" [3], an apple green [4] picked out with black lines [3, 4]. Engine names were in light yellow [3] unless incorporated in cast plates; one engine for example had its name, *Fowler* painted on the leading splashers, and the legend L & S W R CO./ENGINEER'S DEPT. on the rear ones [5]. This livery presumably fell into disuse when the ballast engines were taken into the normal locomotive stock in 1888, but it seems possible that the green livery may have been the origin of Adams' new standard engine livery of 1885. An exception to the above livery was *Mina,* a 0-4-0ST bought in 1874, which was at first black [6] but later dark green [6], a change probably coinciding with its rebuilding in 1882 [7]. This engine had red connecting and coupling rods [6].

5.2 L S W R Engineer's Department rolling stock

The ordinary ballast wagons at the end of the pre-grouping period were painted red oxide [8]. Otherwise they were marked similarly to goods wagons (see Section 4.3). Examples of the markings of ballast wagons [9] and ballast brakes [9, 10] are shown in figs. 20 a-f, k, l. N.b., fig. 20 does not purport to indicate that the wagon strapping was coloured differently to the planking, and the same reservation applies to figs. 15 and 16. The steel ballast hopper wagons of 1898 [11] and the associated ballast ploughs [12] were painted a dark colour, probably red oxide as used later on the first series of bogie hopper wagons [13, 14]. The makers' photograph of the four- and eight wheeled hoppers, and the ballast ploughs, show that the lettering was of an unusual form, characterised by flat-topped letter S, and it is suggested that this happened because of incomplete specification of the form of the letters by the L S W R; the same thing happened with some S R wagons thirty years later on — perhaps the same set of stencils were still in use in the drawing office. The same makers' photographs also show the principal lettering on the hopper wagons to have been shaded, but this too appears to have been quite unofficial.

5.3 Internal use wagons.

A note in the Company minutes laid down that vehicles for internal use in Southampton docks were to be painted red [15]. Some ballast wagons had white circles painted at the right end of the side as shown in figs. 20d-f [9]. As a similar marking appears to be present on an L S W R tarpaulin shown in a 1911 photograph of the docks [16], it is suggested that this was an internal use mark.

5.4 Breakdown vehicles.

Riding vans from 1912 onwards were likely to have carried numbers with a suffix s [17]. The Bournemouth riding van c. 1920 appears to have been an ordinary passenger brake with BOURNEMOUTH/CENTRAL painted in white in the waist panel of the ducket [18]. The Nine Elms breakdown crane of c. 1905 was known as "Red Rover", which presumably indicates its colour [19].

5.5 S R Engineer's Department rolling stock.

The basic L S W R livery of red oxide with white lettering was perpetuated [20]. Numbering was in the main S R series and the old L S W R number plates were again turned round as on ordinary goods stock (fig. 20g [21]). This scheme continued until nationalisation on the various sorts of small bottom-door ballast wagons used by the S R [22], with the usual adjustments of the presentation of the lettering in 1936. The bogie hopper wagons are believed to have followed suit. Ballast brakes also continued to be painted red oxide, with lettering as shown in fig. 20m [9] and bright red ends in the fashion of ordinary goods brakes [10].

5.6 Other departmental vehicles.

The normal colouring for tool vans etc. was the dark grey (approximately no. 632 of BS 381C:1964) used by the Civil Engineer's Department, but as noted in Section 6.8, this shade faded considerably in service with long exposure and lack of renewal, so that in extreme cases towards nationalisation the peeling remnants were almost white [22]. Fig. 20p [23] shows a normal arrangement of the lettering, which was white, on an ex-L S W R flower van, while fig. 20n [23] shows what was probably a very early interpretation of the scheme. Fig. 20h [24] shows the Exmouth Junction tool van with lettering of the 1936 layout on a very faded grey finish; this vehicle had a cast numberplate (possibly drawn here too small) of a type which was evidently produced at Ashford works during the grouping period for both traffic [23] and departmental vehicles. Some vans were transferred to service use without repainting, and fig. 20j [22] shows one such, a much faded tool van allocated to Yeovil Town shed (see also Section 4.7, ref. 47).

A rather exceptional van was no. 993S (fig. 20q [25]), which was refurbished in full passenger livery (except for lining) and endorsed, probably in yellow, for the use of the Chief Mechanical Engineer. This van acquired a condemnation marking, a red stencilled saltire, which was also applied to a more normally marked van of this type, no. 1494S. The latter, apparently painted grey, was inscribed LOCOMOTIVE/RUNNING /DEPT../SHARNAL STREET in the left end panel, and had 9 in. Company initials in the centre, with the small legend TOOL VAN 1494S/X astride the brake-shaft bracket; the number was marked in the eaves panels [23].

The grey scheme extended to cranes. For example, the Bournemouth coal crane, no. 60S (later DS 60), was plain grey with red buffer beams [26].

References

1. Ellis, C. H., *The South Western Railway,* London, George Allen and Unwin, 1956, p. 107.
2. Thompson, W. B., in *Railway Magazine,* v. 63, p. 408 (Nov. 1928).
3. *Locomotive Magazine,* v. 36, p. 386 (15th Nov. 1930).
4. Bradley, D. L., *Locomotives of the London and South Western Railway,* Solihull, Railway Correspondence and Travel Society, 1965, p. 124.
5. Ibid., p. 127.
6. Bushell, A. M., in *Railway Magazine,* v. 63, p. 408 (Nov. 1928).
7. Bradley, op. cit., p. 125.
8. Hemingway, G. Y., HMRS drawing no. 16 W 495, 10 ton 15 ft. 3 in. drop-side wagon no. 300. Mr Tumilty points out that this is not an Engineer's Department vehicle, since it is neither so marked nor does it bear the normal plate inscribed ENGINEER'S DEPT./999/L & S W R, but its place seems to be in this Section.

9. After drawings prepared for the Society by H. V. Tumilty and based on photographs of c. 1918.
10. Newton, J., drawing no. SWC/D/1 printed with notes by A. Blackburn in *Model Railway Constructor,* v. 31, p. 270 (Oct. 1964).
11. Photograph, R. Y. Pickering & Co. collection.
12. Photograph, Hurst, Nelson & Co. collection.
13. Photograph in *Railway Magazine,* v. 28, p. 477, (June 1911).
14. Edwards Bros. drawing.
15. BTHR.
16. In the Maritime Museum, Southampton.
17. BTHR.
18. Ellis, op. cit., photograph f.p. 177.
19. Box, F. E., MS note in scrapbook now in the collection of Mr. N. Pattenden.
20. Allen, P. C. and Macleod, A. B., *Rails in the Isle of Wight,* London, George Allen and Unwin, 1967, p. 58.
21. Newton, J., drawing no. SWC/D/3 printed in *Model Railway Constructor,* v. 32, p. 14 (Jan. 1965).
22. The writer, noted c. 1950-1.
23. Based upon a photograph.
24. Measured details taken in 1951.
25. Measured details and paint fragments from grounded body at Wickham (see also Appendix 2.7).
26. The writer, noted in September 1967, when the crane was broken up.

Section 6 — Buildings and structures

6.1 The period before 1890.

Very little information has come to light about the colouring of early L S W R buildings—apart from that of the masonry or brick of which they were built. The few photographs of the period show paintwork which is arguably similar to that of the years after 1890, i.e. a light stone colour for the body of buildings, with darker corner posts. This is confirmed by a painting, believed to be an authentic record of Blechynden station c. 1890 [1]. There are, however, three paint fragments (see Appendices 2.13, 2.14 and 2.15) which probably date back to c. 1880 and include dark reddish brown colours. These may only be undercoats, and it happens that all three samples have been taken off ironwork, but it is possible that they represent a finish colour which was similiar to that of the early locomotives.

Colour:

Grayish red	7·5 R 2/4 [2]
Moderate reddish brown	7·5 R 3/6 [3, 4]

Plates 5a and b in this book show the use of a three-tone colour scheme on the new awnings at Basingstoke. It was from the capital of one of the pillars on the left in plate 5b that the paint sample described [4] was obtained. In contrast to later practice, all the roof ironwork is apparently brown, and there do not seem to be any nameboards, although in lieu of them there is a very prominent sign reading GENTLEMEN.

A very early note in the minutes of the Locomotive and Way and Works Committee [5] specifies the protective treatment to be applied to the carriage sheds ordered on 2nd July 1847 to be erected at some stations on the Dorchester line. Half of these sheds were to be sheeted with galvanised corrugated iron, and the rest with plain corrugated iron painted with Lithic paint. According to a much later source [6], this paint was "a mastic of petalite (which contains an alkali known as lithia) sand and litharge used as a coating for walls", which description suggests a light buff colour.

6.2 From 1890 to the grouping.

The painting of L S W R buildings seems to have been consistently on the following principles, which amount to the use of three different shades of brown.

Colours:

A: **Pinkish buff** Appendix 1.18

Pinkish buff like the carriage upper quarters but rather lighter [7]

Much the same pinky-brown as the carriages, but pinker [8]

Stone or dark buff, weathering to pinkish buff [9]

Moderate yellowish pink	2·5 YR 7/4 [10]
Moderate yellowish pink	**2·5 YR 8/4** [11] (close to ★ 17)
Light orange	**2·5 YR 8/6** [11] (close to ★ 17)
Light brown	5 YR 5/5 [12]
Brownish orange	5 YR 5/8 [12]
Moderate orange	5 YR 7/6 [11]
Light orange	5 YR 8/4 [11]
Light orange	5 YR 8/7 [11]
Moderate yellowish pink	5 YR 8/8 [11]

B: *Pale stone* Appendix 1.19

Very pale cream [7]

Pale orange yellow	**7·5 YR 9/4** [11]
Light orange yellow	10 YR 9/6 [13]

C: *Dark brown* Appendix 1.20

Dark brown [14]

Umber [9]

	Dark brown, no. 3-039 of BS 2660:1955	**5 YR 1·5/4** [11]
	Moderate brown	5 YR 3/3 [4]
	Moderate brown	5 YR 4/5 [13]
	Moderate brown	7·5 YR 3/4 [15]
	Moderate brown	7·5 YR 4/5 [15]
D:	Light green [9]	
	Very pale green	2·5 G 9/2 est. [11]
	Very light yellowish green	**2·5 G 9/3** [4]
E:	Red [9]	
F:	Grey [7]	
	Medium gray	**N 5** [2]
	Light gray	N 7 [3]

A wooden building might be painted overall in the pinkish buff (A) — and Ellis states that this accords with the recollection of his father, who was born in 1864 [7]—but usually there were two shades of the basic colour, such parts as corner posts and door frames being darker than the rest. Judging from photographs, combinations both of B with A and A with C were used, but in view of the wide range of shades which colour A could take on, it seems likely that the same state of affairs existed on the L S W R as on the G W R, and that the local paint foreman mixed the colours to his own personal interpretation of Company instructions [16]. If this was the case, it becomes rather unrealistic to speak of a livery as such; the colour of the paintwork was about as fixed as the colour of the bricks used up and down the system — with the one proviso that the finished job would look earthy. Indeed, one of the characteristics of 19th century house-painting must have been its reliance on orange, brown and dark red pigments. The L S W R and S R present a neat case of the transition from reliance on earth pigments to the general use of the products of the chemical industry. Adams' introduction of a bright green for the engines was followed by a similar change in respect of carriages in 1915, and buildings followed suit at the grouping. So too, hand mixed paints, apparently with no varnish content (they "turned darker when rained upon" [7]) were superseded by canned high gloss.

A brick or stone building would have the fixed portions of window frames in colour A, dark brown (C) doors with A-colour panels [9] and perhaps dark brown barge-boards [17], but stuccoed buildings were given a wash of colour A with window frames, reveals and surrounds, barge boards and water pipes in dark brown (plate 6b) [18]. The awning attached to a station building was usually painted pinkish buff with dark brown mouldings (including the triangular decoration on the end gable) [9], but a band of lighter colour sometimes appeared between two mouldings along the platform face of the awning, and there was a very widespread practice of painting alternate vertical planks of the awning in different shades of stone. Plate 6a shows a rather extreme case of this, and it seems likely that the darker of the two colours on the awning was a brown rather than a stone colour; but the lighter colour can be seen to be darker than the planking of the signal box. Similar striped painting was indulged in by the painters on many pre-grouping railways, and was to be seen on many other buildings of the time. Present-day football stand colours are perhaps a last vestige of the practice!

Ironwork supporting awnings was pale green [4], while the main pillars were dark brown [9]. But some photographs show a change of colour about two feet from the top of the pillar, rather as if the painter had been allowing for the addition of the familiar, ornate cast-iron brackets. The bases of awning pillars are stated to have been black, with a red ring separating the black and brown areas [9], but unfortunately the colours are not distinguishable in photographs, owing to the characteristics of contemporary film emulsions and this point is completely unconfirmed.

A few buildings seem to have been dark brown all over; the old (*very* old) signal box at Brockenhurst (the "A" box, which in L S W R days was called Brockenhurst East) showed during its demolition in 1964 that its main planking had been, in part at least, painted dark brown, and no. 7 crossing-keeper's house nearby also had its red and white brickwork painted this colour [19]. Such things as platform fencing and seats [7], lamp posts and advertisement boards were also dark brown [7, 17], but some board fencing was buff [7] and the rougher fences were merely creosoted (this applied to sleeper, post and rail and lattice fences) [7, 17].

Footbridges, however, showed considerable variation. The older wooden examples were treated [17] in at least three ways, viz.:

(i) all buff, e.g. at Andover.
(ii) mainly dark brown with lighter members and cross bracing in buff, e.g. Wadebridge.
(iii) main members buff, with lighter members pale stone and handrails dark brown, e.g. Brockenhurst.

Steel footbridges were grey [3] ("latterly" says Ellis [7]). Lattice bridges generally appear to have been very dark (brown?) while the plate type were of a lighter shade. The elegant type built around two columns made from heavy, bent rolled steel joists (which is most common on the Southampton-Portsmouth and Brockenhurst-Bournemouth lines) was perhaps painted stone colour [17].

6.3 Station nameboards may have been subject to local taste for a long time (with the qualification noted in Section 6.1), but standardisation was enforced in 1906. Of the unstandardised boards the following details are known.

(i) Brockenhurst: Very large pale board with dark (brown?) block letters shaded to the right in a light colour and underneath in a darker (buff?): BROCKENHURST,/CHANGE FOR/LYMINGTON. The posts and surround of the board were apparently in dark brown and stone as later [20].
(ii) Bournemouth (Central): Apparently black letters, shaded to the left in white (?) and underneath in a medium (stone?) colour. The main panel was probably light stone and the posts and framing dark brown. This extended on to the board to form a broad margin and was scalloped in the corners, similarly to
(iii) Parkstone: where large panels of what was apparently A-coloured paint were applied to the brick staircases of the footbridge (see fig. 21k [19]).

(iv) Egloskerry: enamelled iron signs; 10¼ in. white block lettering on dark mauvy blue ground [21]. Similar signs appeared at Launceston, Tresmeer and Fort Brockhurst [17], and the colouring — B.S. no. 108, 7·5 PB 2·5/10 — was also noted on the car stop boards introduced in 1915 for the London area electric services and eventually used also on the stations served by the Portsmouth electrification scheme (see (figs. 21f-j [19]).

(v) Whitstone and Bridgerule: enamelled iron signs with black letters on a white ground [21].

The 1906 specification seems to have been an attempt to economise on signwriting costs, and was associated with the introduction of standard cast-iron or wood letters which were used to form the inscription in a form which could easily be painted legibly by comparatively unskilled painters. The posts and framework were dark brown, the surround moulding was buff, the main ground of the board pale stone and the letters themselves were black [22]. This colouring also seems to have been used for bridge number plates figs 22d, e [23,24] and the nameplates of signal boxes — but Earlsfield box, being large and painted pale stone in the main, simply had the usual cut-out letters forming the name attached to the planking below the gallery, and painted black [17]. However, Esher West, a similar box, had a normal, separate nameboard which it retained until, in 1939 or '40, the anonymity campaign claimed it [25]. The normal size of lettering was 9 in. high for the platform boards and 7 in. high for the names on signal boxes, but a larger size also existed, and as fig. 21a [19] shows, this was by no means limited to larger stations. Nameboards were of many different forms of construction although the superficial appearance might be the same; further examples are drawn in figs. 21b [19], c, d (both from Holsworthy, platform and signal box respectively [21]) and e (Bude [21]). Note the apparent adoption of a standard height above the platform surface.

6.4 Miscellaneous features of station painting included the following:

Lamp standards, although usually dark brown in their smaller sizes [7], were pinkish buff with the lower four feet or so brown if they were more than about twelve feet high; lamps painted in this way included those on the platforms at Salisbury, and those in the yards at Southampton and Exeter [17].

Level crossing gates were pinkish buff [7, 17], and had red targets (which were smaller and mounted higher than the currently familiar S R ones). One photograph, taken at Mortlake after 1915 (and thus probably after the war) shows crossing gates of which the meeting styles were painted white. This seems to have been a relic of the first world war black-out. But a different impression of the treatment of crossing gates is given by two less explicit sources. The better evidence is that obtained [19] from examination of some large (iron) level crossing gates adjacent to the former Gosport station; these were probably erected c. 1880 and seem always to have been painted white. They have plain red targets which are obviously local additions to the design, being of odd trapezoidal shapes clipped to the framework (plate (6c). The associated gates across the footway have plain rectangular boards. The second source, the painting previously referred to [1], shows dark brown gates with small rectangular warning boards depending from the top rails of the gates and meeting to form an approximate square of colour. Warning notices of the cast type (fig. 22a, b, c, [26]) appear to have been painted red and white [26] although in contrast to the practice of the S R, the letters were red on a white ground and not the reverse [17].

Structures such as turntables, water tanks and water columns, and steel and iron bridges were simply finished in grey [2, 3, 7, 19].

6.5 A few parts of the **permanent way** were coloured. The working faces of buffer stops were usually striped in the fashion still familiar on the Southern Region of British Railways; the earliest photograph showing this appears to be one dating from c. 1905. Horizontal stripes of white-red-white were used on the front face of the beam, and the rest of the stop was usually black. Hand point levers seem to have been white; the type with a counterweight had one half of the weight painted red [17] — probably this was the half which was uppermost when the switch was reversed. This feature was advertised by Messrs, Ransomes and Rapier as early as 1887 [27].

Ballast was, until the opening of Meldon Quarry in the 1900s, gravel of about 1 in. screen with a distinct yellow appearance [1], as has become apparent in the course of the extensive track relaying operations connected with the Bournemouth electrification scheme [19].

The ends of conductor rails and their protective boards were painted white in the early days of the electric services [28], but the L S W R does not seem to have put the white line along the platform edge during the Great War; this task was left to fall to the Southern, twenty-five years later.

6.6 Building interiors.

The colours used for interior decoration seem to have been muted orange and brown shades [11], or on one account, pink [29], probably much the same as the exterior colours. But the L S W R indulged in many touches of ostentation. Stained glass was sometimes used in the windows (e.g. at Bodmin [21]). Tiles in the Company colours, or at any rate approximations to engine green, goods green, salmon and coach brown might be used on the walls of a refreshment room (e.g. at Yeovil Junction [19]), to form that vanished stand-by of the decorator, a dado. In less opulent places, one in plain dark brown was used. Such a scheme was violently exposed by the bombing in 1940 of the hostel attached to the refreshment rooms at Clapham Junction (main line side). There the colours seemed identical to the old coaching stock colours [14]. On the completely utilitarian side of the tracks, the interiors of goods and locomotive sheds were whitewashed [17].

6.7 Southern Railway schemes.

As far as can be said from the evidence, the painting schemes used by the S R did not change over the whole of the grouping period — and in fact the S R colours continued in use well into the British Railways era, when they were replaced by the nearest B S equivalents, But the S R colours may themselves have been chosen from an early British Standard list, in common with some of the S R goods wagon colours. The basis of the scheme was a buff shade which appears to have been close to the basic L S W R buildings colour (A of Section 6.2), but this was gradually changed to a distinct yellow colour. With the buff colour was used a dark green in place of the dark brown of the L S W R. However, both these colours were subject to considerable discolouration: the buff often gradually acquired a filthy brown appearance, probably from tarry fumes emitted by engines; this was especially the case on station awnings, while the green, unless it turned blue as it often did on the sunward side of buildings and near the sea, got darker and darker with grime, particularly at places where people's clothing or hands rubbed against it.

Colours:

A: *S R no. 1, Light stone*
Used for valance interior, roof interior, interior walls, upper parts of buildings free standing under awnings, standard timber gates, close boarded fence. Replaced by grayish yellow, no. 386 of BS 381C:1948
10 YR 8/4 est. [30]

B: Predominant colour
SR no. 1A, Dark stone

Light brown	5 YR 5/5 [12]
Moderate orange yellow	7·5 YR 8/8 [31]
Light yellowish brown	**10 YR 7/5** [10] ★ 18
Moderate orange yellow	10 YR 8/6 [15]

Used for valance exterior, lavatory entrance screens, wooden walls, signal box planking and balustrades, close-boarded fencing, paled gates, open pale fences (unless creosoted — thus not on platforms), barge boards of corrugated iron huts.
Replaced by moderate orange yellow, no. 358 of BS 381C:1948 10 YR 7/7 [30]

C: *SR no. 2, White*
Used for window sashes, ceilings (water paint), flag poles, level crossing gates, wicket gates, railings at bridge approaches, discretionary for standard timber gates in lieu of A [30].

D: *SR no. 3, Dark green*
Used for 4 in. border on poster boards. Replaced by dark yellowish green no. 276 of BS 381C : 1948 2·5 G 3/4 est. [30]

E: Predominant colour
SR no. 3A, Mid chrome green

Dark yellowish green	10 GY 4/5 [12, 13] discolouring to
Grayish olive green	5 GY 3/2 [13]
Dark yellowish green	2·5 G 4/6 [2]
Strong yellowish green	2·5 G 5/8 [15]
Strong green	5 G 5/7 [3]
Strong green	5 G 5/8 [32]
Strong bluish green	10 G 5/8 [2]

Used for valance mouldings, drain pipes, awning columns, handrails and railings, window frames, internal walls up to 4 ft. from the floor, plus 1¼ in. band, building corner posts and plinths, doors and frames, metal fittings, signal box handrails (wood and iron), capping of close-boarded fencing, metal gates and fences, corrugated iron fences, grounded bodies in station limits, signal/telephone boxes, gables above water tanks (?), buffer stop structure in vicinity of platforms [30], metal lamp posts [14].
This colour has been carried forwards into B R days, a major supplier being British Paints Ltd., who designate the colour as *Superlative Brilliant Green* [14], a title embodying the B S name for:
Deep yellowish green, no. 221 of BS 381C: 1964 10 GY 4/8 [30]

F: *SR no. 4, Light green*

Strong yellowish green	7·5 GY 6/7 [4]
Light yellowish green	10 GY 8/7 [4] discolouring to
Light olive	10 Y 5/5 [4]
Pale green	2·5 G 6/2 [11]

Used for roofing steelwork and ornamental brackets.
Replaced by moderate yellow green, no. 217 of BS 381C:1964 7·5 GY 6/6 [30]

G: *SR no. 6, Black*
Used for metalwork of level crossing gates [30]

H: *SR no. 7, Pale green*
Replaced by moderate yellowish green, no. 275 of BS 381C:1964 2·5 G 6·5/4 [30]

J: *SR no. 8, Grey*

Light gray	N 7 [2, 3]
Light gray	N 8 [3]

Used for signal box walkways, exposed point levers, gutter interiors, top of corrugated iron awnings, poster board centres, grounded bodies outside station limits, water tanks, ladders, water columns,
Replaced by dark bluish gray, no. 632 of BS 381C : 1964 10B 4/0·5 [30]

K: *SR no. 9, Red*
Used for targets of level crossing gates, fire buckets and cupboards, hose carts.
Replaced by vivid red, no. 538 of BS 381C: 1964 S R 3·5/16 [30]

L: *SR no. 10, Deep cream*
Used for internal walls (upper part plus 2 in. band), ceilings if coved to walls.
Replaced by moderate yellow, no. 352 of BS 381C:1964 4 Y 8/5 [30]

6.8 Wartime changes.

Paint samples and photographs indicate no change in basic painting during the war, when maintenance was reduced to a minimum. Copious white markings were painted on corners and pillars of buildings to aid those groping in the black-out; the rule seems to have been 9 in. bands of white, 9 in. apart, with one band at eye-level and as many as convenient below that. Overhead glass should have been replaced by board or painted black, and steel sheeting put up around signal box windows were dark gray [14].

A small number of important buildings were actually camouflaged, in an attempt to protect them from air attack. Buildings concerned were (i) repair works (presumably including Eastleigh, Brighton and Ashford), (ii) goods sheds (Fratton being so identified), (iii) carriage sheds (Wimbledon and Fratton being known) (iv) electric power station (Durnsford Road) and sub-stations (apparently throughout the Southern electric system) and (v) stations (only two identified: Hamble halt and Hillsea halt, both of which were close by aircraft factories and erected 1942), All these buildings were made to take on the visual texture of their neighbourhoods, although the depot at Fratton was made to look like a clump of trees [19, 33].

6.9 Station nameboards, and other display writing.

The Southern initially used the old L S W R nameboards, repainting them in due course with white letters on a green ground or red, if the message was cautionary, (and occasionally making new cast notice boards with its own name in place of the South Western initials [19]). But from around 1930 the S R started to use a distinctive alphabet on enamelled signs. As remarked in Section 2.13, this was an attempt to create a house style and was based on the use of the Company's title written in bold letters approximately of the style called "Gill sans", which had been adopted by the L N E R in 1928 [34]. Perhaps to stress its individuality, the S R at first formed the letters with all the ends of strokes rounded off instead of being square cut. This appears to have been a short-lived style, for examples are now very rare [35], and the usual presentation was in the form shown in fig. 22f [36] and plate 7c. The internal line in each letter in the same colour as the ground, was invariable in both forms of the lettering (it seems easier to think of this construction rather than of letters with outlines). As noted in Section 2.13, the form of the letter N was modified after a while also, and an example is shown in plate 7d. Another borrowing, this time from the Underground of London, was the design of station nameplates shown in fig. 21. 1 [37]. In these, the lettering and segments were (and mostly still are) white, and the background green (approximately dark yellowish green, no. 282 of BS 381C:1964 10 GY 3·5/4 [37]). This sort of sign has a long history, since having been adapted by the Underground from an American prototype, it passed to the S R and thence, by a heraldic mutation caused by early London Transport influence at BTC headquarters [38], gave the "starving lion" adopted by B R in 1948, and still lingers in the revised totem which was standard until the professional designers caught up with it in 1964. After that, graphically speaking, B R didn't know which way it was going. The modification of the S R alphabet can be followed in such things as posters (plates 8b, c) and system maps; indeed a survey of railway publicity material from a design point of view would be a useful exercise. Plate 7b shows another link with print; the phrase SOUTHERN ELECTRIC, with the flash, featured in the maps referred to. Larger-size station nameboards were turned out in hundreds; those made by the S R which still remain can be distinguished from the generally similar BR productions by the fact that the latter use a genuine Gill sans alphabet [38].

References

1. In the Tudor House Museum, Southampton. See Tavender, L., in *HMRS Journal*, v. 6, pp. 148-50. (1969).
2. Paint fragment described in Appendix 2.13.
3. Paint fragment described in Appendix 2.14.
4. Paint fragment described in Appendix 2.15.
5. BTHR LSW 1/174, entry no. 259, 20th July 1847.
6. Knight, —, *Dictionary of Mechanics*, 1875, quoted in *New English Dictionary*, s.v. Lithic.
7. Ellis, C. H., private communication of recollections of his father and himself.
8. Ellis, C. H., *The South Western Railway*, London, George Allen and Unwin, 1956, p. 24.
9. Abbott, N. L., private communication quoting ex-L S W R painter.
10. Paint fragment described in Appendix 2.16.
11. Paint fragments described in Appendix 2.17.
12. Paint fragments described in Appendix 2.18.
13. Paint fragments described in Appendix 2.21.
14. Turner, J. T. Howard, private communication of recollections and recent notes.
15. Paint fragments described in Appendix 2.19.
16. Slinn, J. N., *HMRS Livery Register no. 2, Great Western Railway*, Reading, Historical Model Railway Society, 1967, p. 26.
17. From study of photographs.
18. Colours of Christchurch old station until its demolition in 1968.
19. The writer, noted 1964-9.
20. Photograph in Haresnape, B., *Railway Design since 1830, vol. 1, 1830-1914*, London, Ian Allan, 1968, fig. 235, p. 126.
21. Tumilty, H. V., private communication of notes c. 1964.
22. *L S W R Specification for the painting of Station Name-Boards*, Engineer's Office, Waterloo, March 1906, quoted by George Dow in *HMRS Journal*, v. 2, pp. 25, 27 (1956).
23. Measured details of plate in a private collection.
24. Adcock, T., measured details of a plate at Swanwick station, 1969.
25. Museum of British Transport photograph no. 221/40.
26. Peacock, C. J., measured details and notes from a plate in his collection.
27. Ransomes and Rapier, Engineers, *Catalogue no. 151*, London, 1887, p. 5.
28. Photograph in Moody, G. T., *Southern Electric 1909-1968*, London, Ian Allan, 1968, p. 10.
29. Collins, J. B. B., in *Railway Magazine*, v. 15, p. 284 (Sept. 1904).

Fig. 14 LSWR and SR wagon lettering

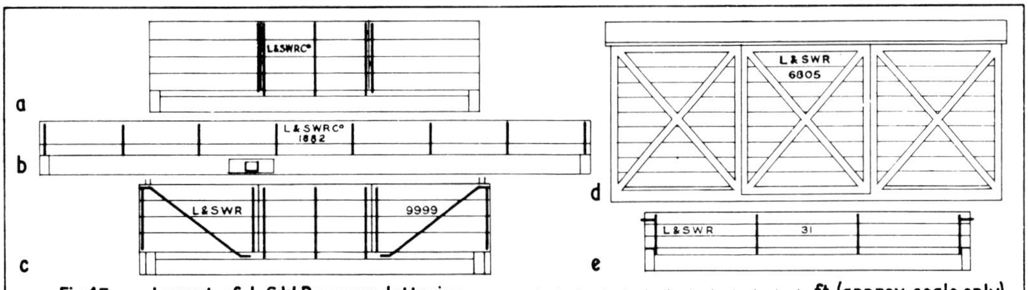

Fig. 15 Layout of LSWR wagon lettering

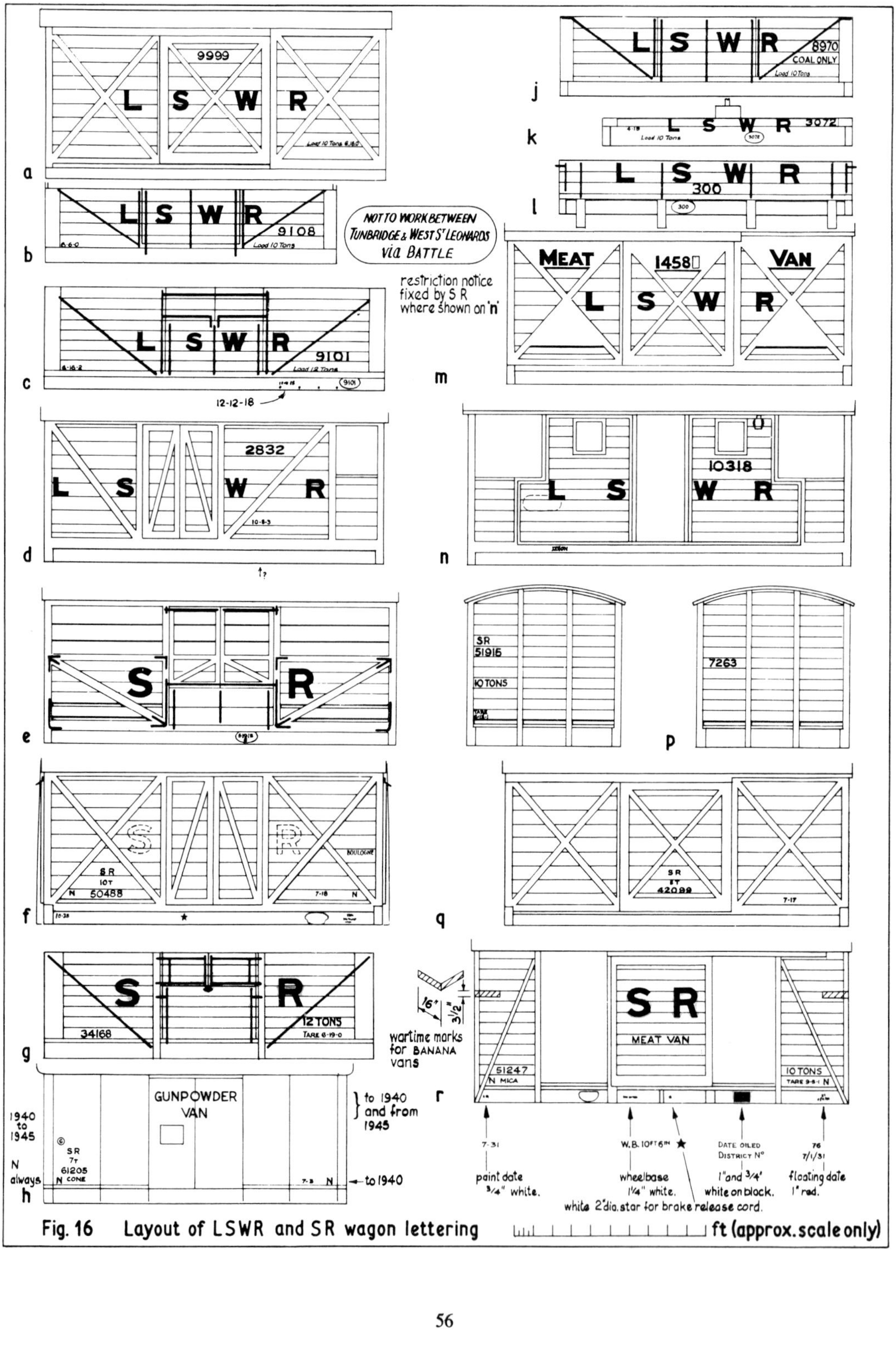

Fig. 16 Layout of LSWR and SR wagon lettering ft (approx. scale only)

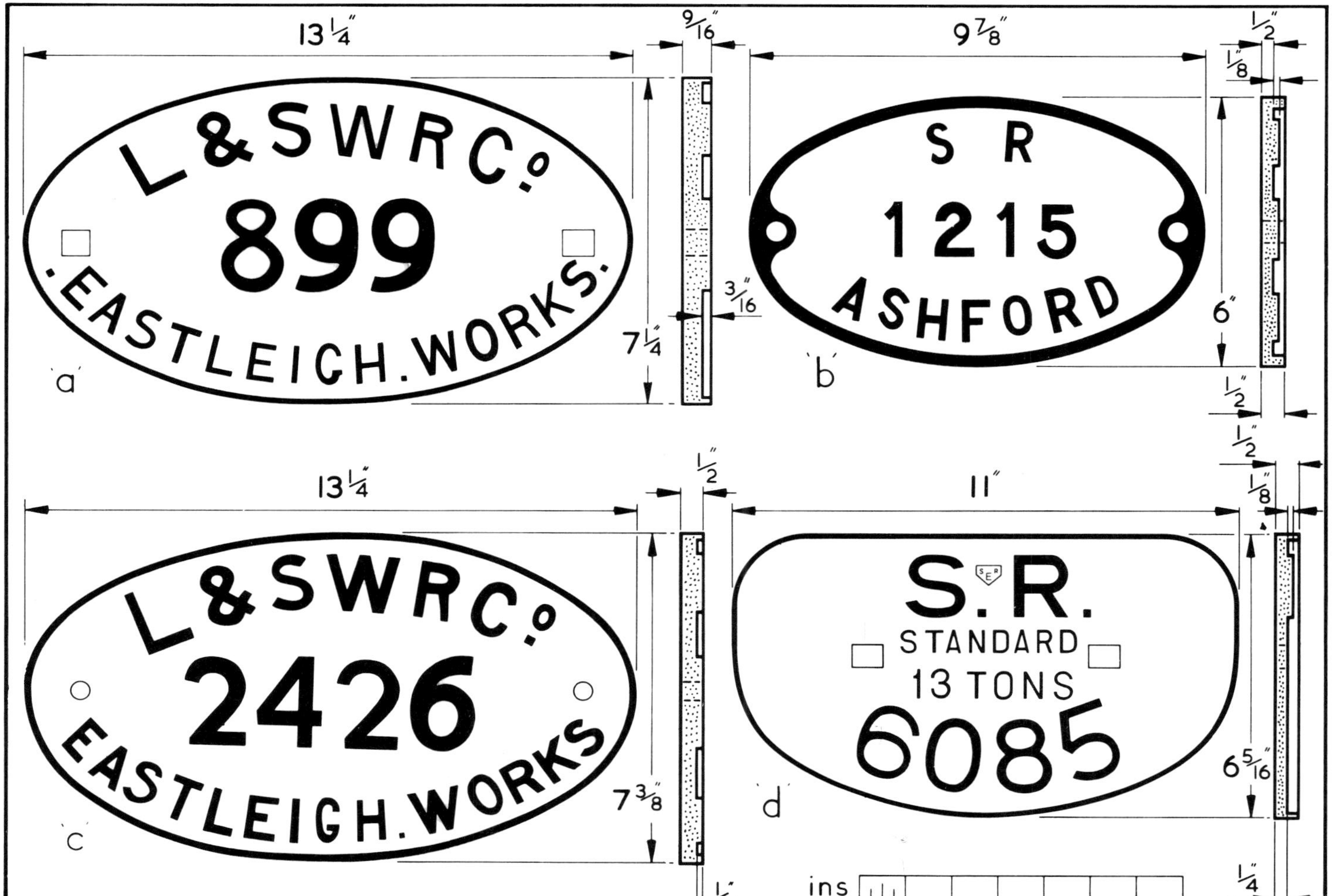

Fig. 17 L S W R and S R wagon number plates

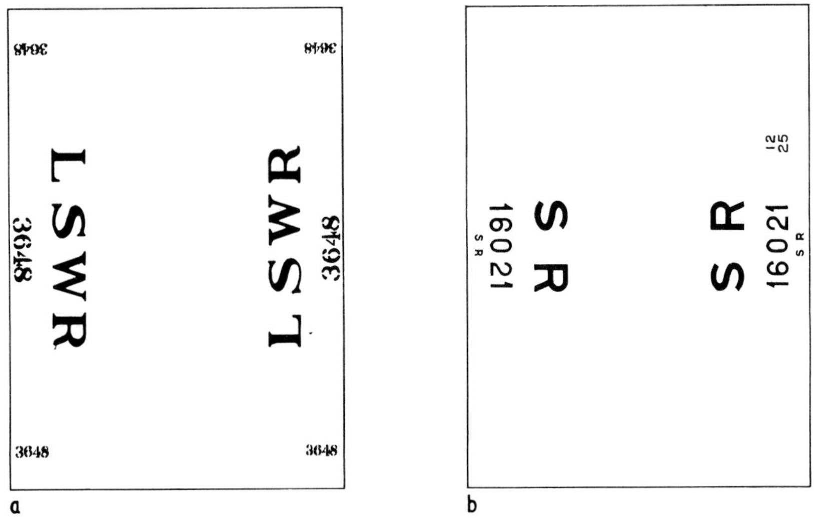

a b

Fig. 18 LSWR and SR wagon tarpaulin lettering

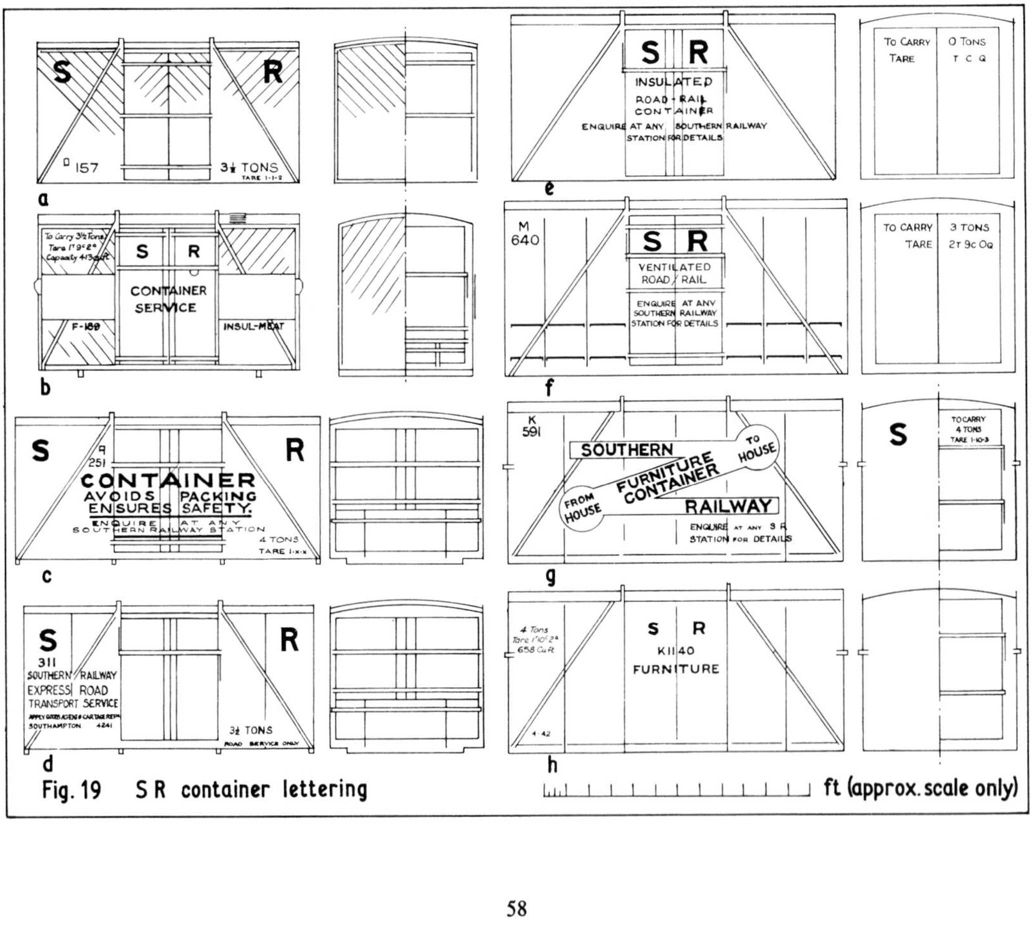

a b c d e f g h

Fig. 19 S R container lettering

ft (approx. scale only)

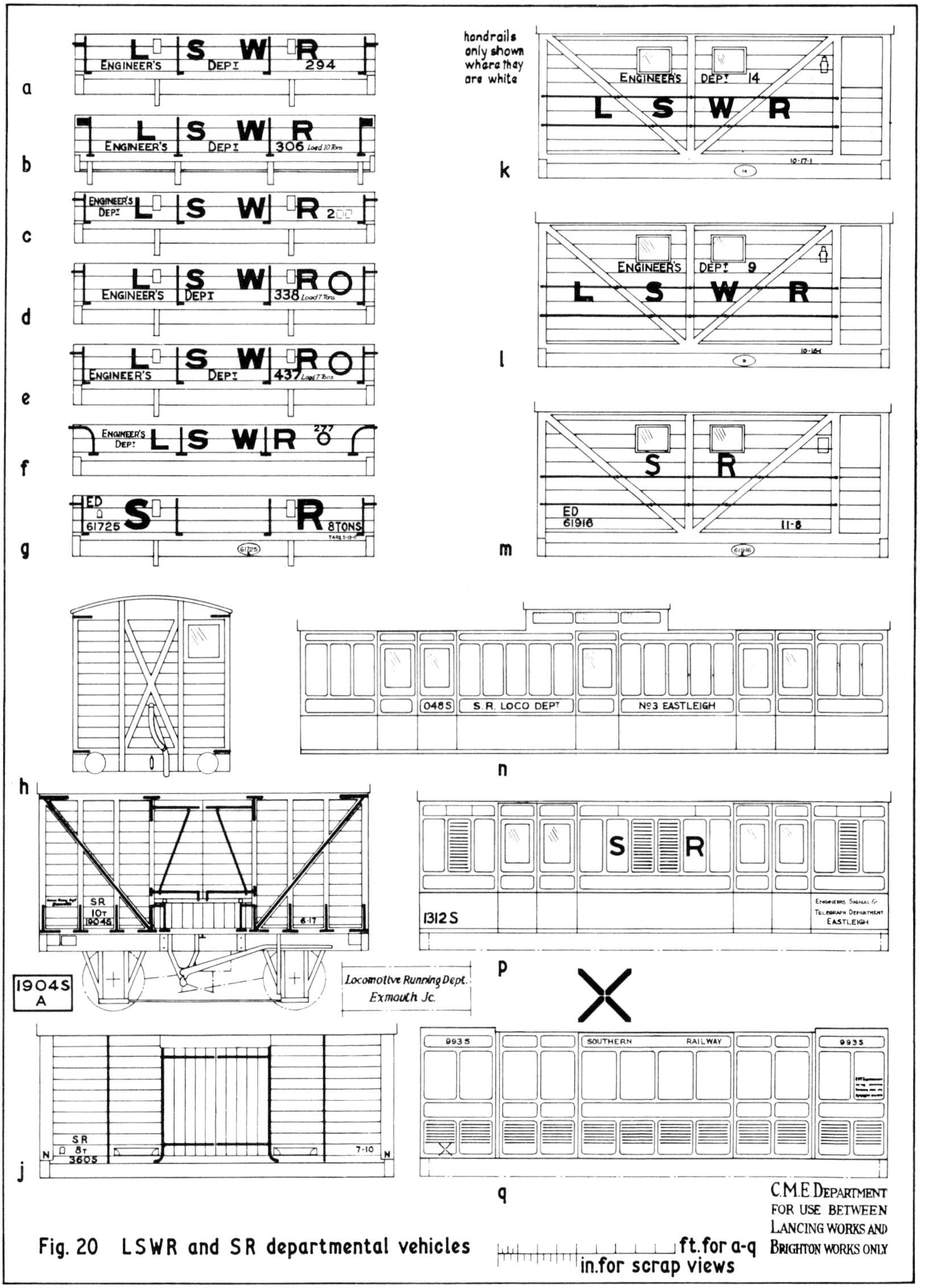

Fig. 20 LSWR and SR departmental vehicles

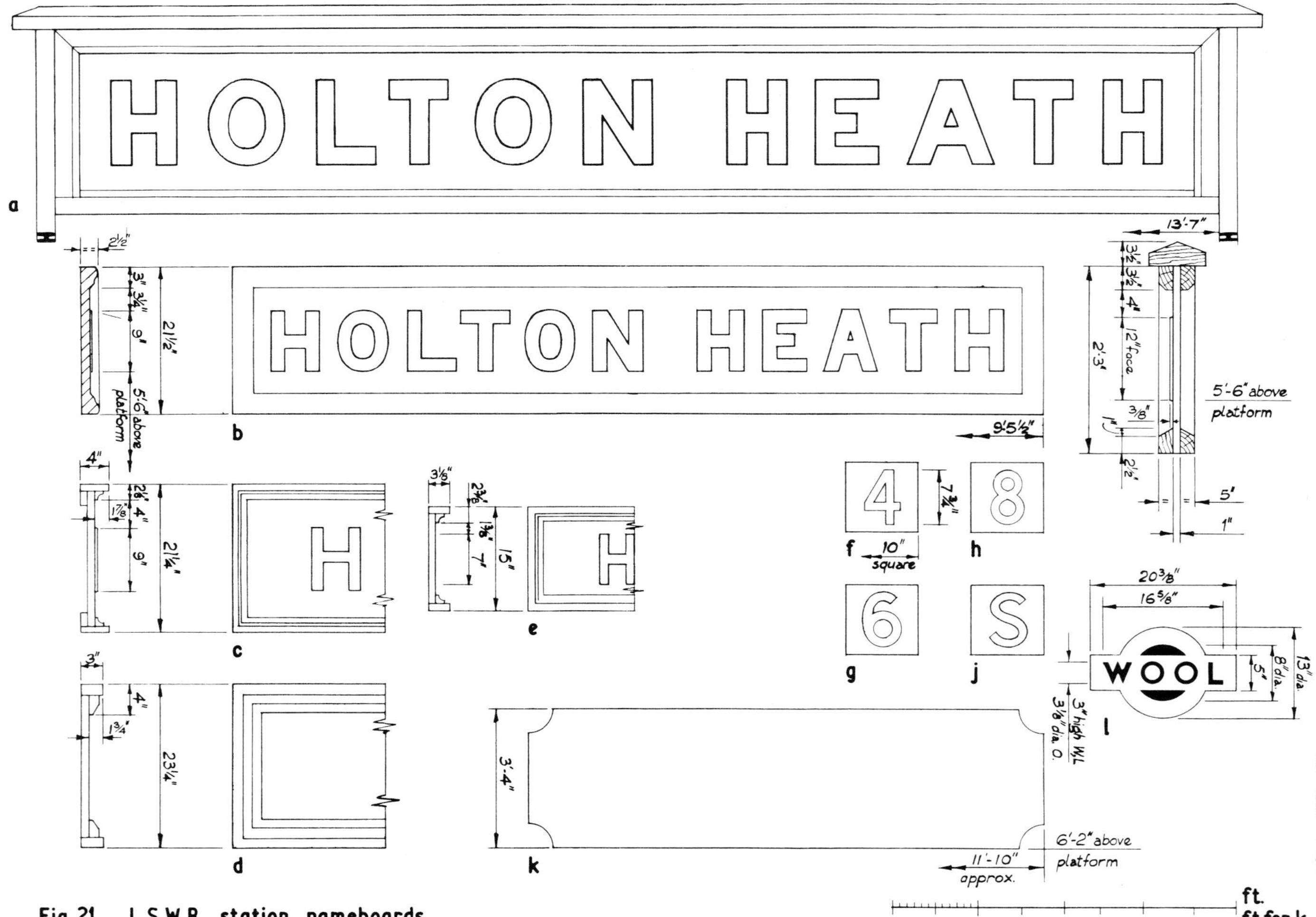

Fig. 21 LSWR station nameboards

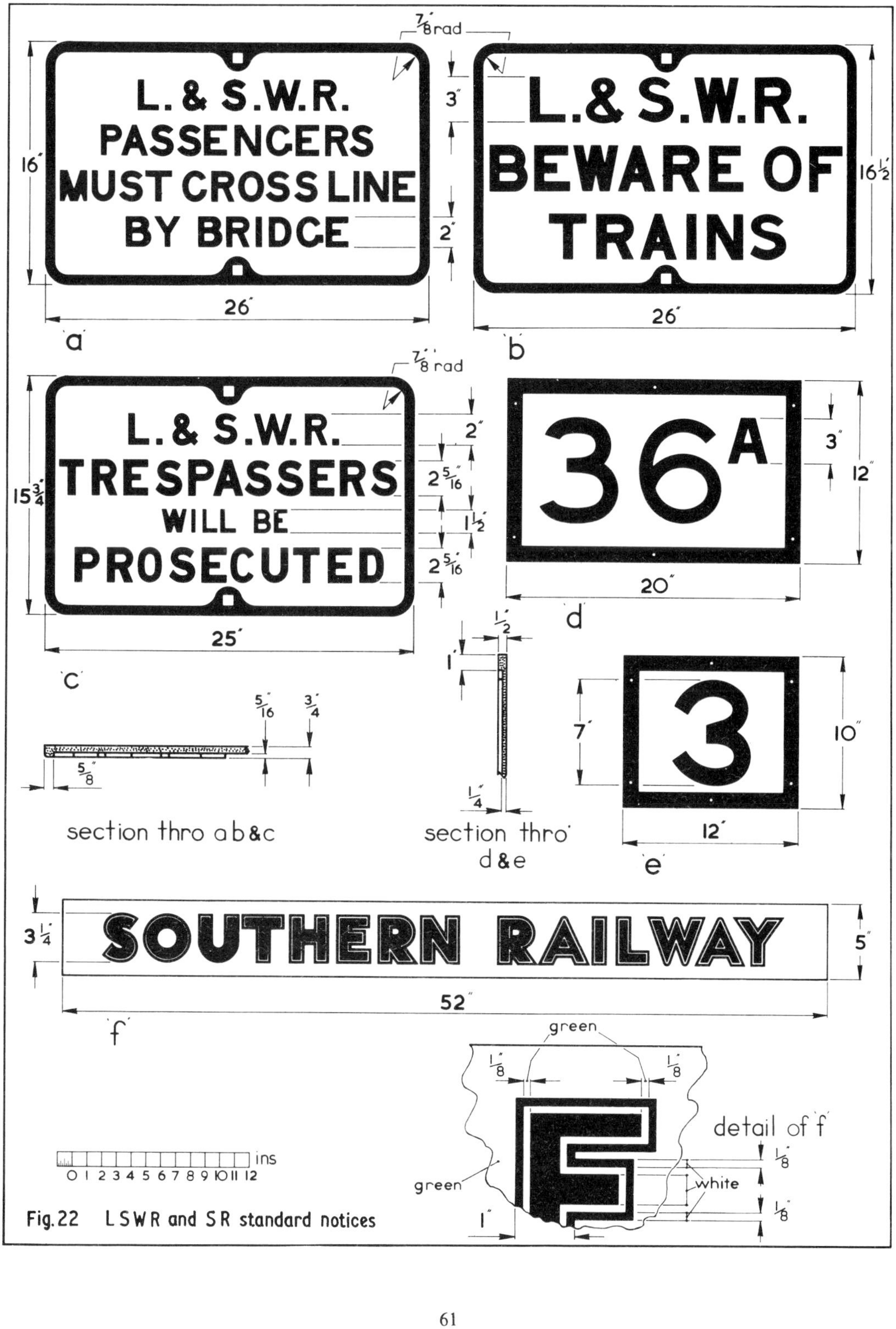

Fig. 22 LSWR and SR standard notices

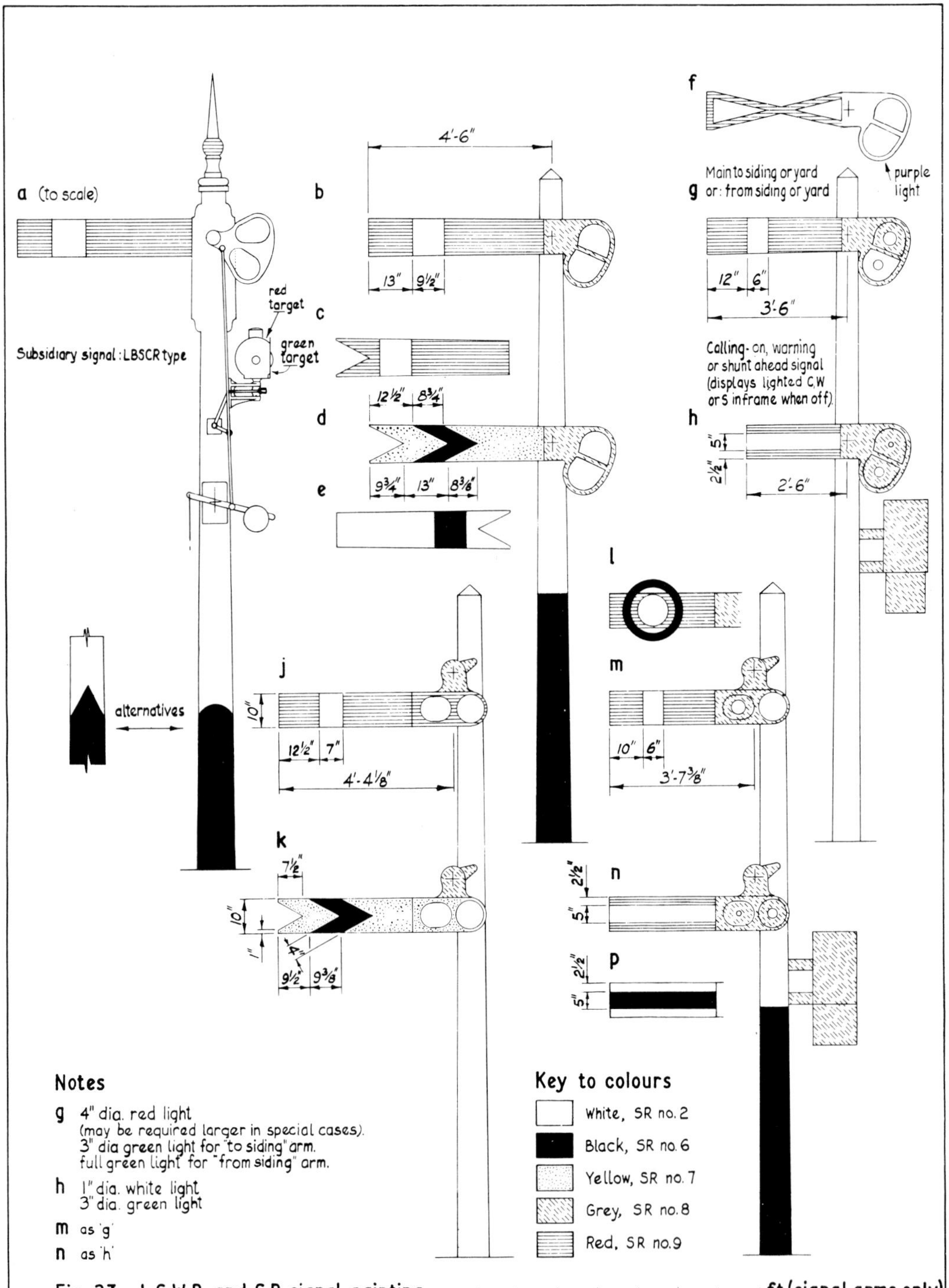

Fig. 23 LSWR and SR signal painting

30. BR-SR CCE Information Sheet BR(s)E/1/etc. (Dec. 1949, reissued as S.02.17.01, etc. in Jan. 1960).
31. Paint fragment described in Appendix 2.20.
32. Paint fragment described in Appendix 2.22.
33. Tavender, L., in *HMRS Journal*, v. 5, pp. 170-1 (1967).
34. Davis, A., in *Design*, no. 171, pp. 72-5 (March 1963).
35. Two enamelled examples only known: a notice board heading and a large plate worded "Great Western and Southern Railways", both formerly at Yeovil Town station.
36. Measured details from a plate in Mr D. W. Knight's collection, formerly at Bude.
37. Measured details from a plate in the writer's collection.
38. Dow, G., private communication.

Section 7 Signals

7.1 Disc signals.

The early signals of the L S W R were of a form introduced by Albinus Martin [1]. The signal consisted of a circular disc four feet in diameter, pivoted at the centre, with a groove around the rim in which ran a cord, by means of which the disc could be rotated. Half the centre of the disc was cut away, so that one half was "solid" while the other half was "open" except for the rim. The pivot was mounted at the top of a post which could itself be turned through a right angle, so that the disc could be turned edge-on so as to be virtually invisible to the drivers of approaching trains. In this position it signified "all clear" for both directions. When turned so that the disc was at right angles to the track, the signal denoted "stop", the line to which it applied being shown by rotating the disc so that when the "solid" half was on the left, the left hand road was blocked (and thus the right-hand one was clear), and vice versa. Rotating the disc so that the "solid" part was above the horizontal axis denoted that both roads were blocked [1].

This type of signal began to be replaced by semaphores in 1863.

The posts were painted white with black bases, sometimes with the top of the black portion curved or pointed on each side of the post [2].

The discs themselves, when used as "station" signals, were painted red on both sides on double main lines [3, 4], whilst branch line signals at junctions had a fixed lower green ring [3]. The grooved rims of the discs were black [3]. When used as "auxiliary" signals (or distants), the working face was red [3] and the back was white [3], and the disc was not rotated but was turned on the post only, to give "clear". The diameter of the disc of "auxiliary" signals was three feet [4].

7.2 Semaphore running signals.

The painting of L S W R semaphores conformed to the normal British practice, the working face being red and the back white. The markings on the arms were normally plain white (on red) and black (on white) stripes, even on distant arms, which only began to be notched later than 1874/5 [2], some time after they were introduced [2] (fig. 23c [5, 6, 7]). The fronts of distant arms began to have white chevrons, in place of white stripes, about 1910 [2] (fig. 23d for sizes). The backs were not altered [2] (fig. 23e [7]).

Yellow distant arms with black chevrons began to be introduced in Southern Railway days, from 1927, in common with practice on the G W R and L N E R [2] (fig. 23d, k [8, 9]). Black chevrons were then painted on the backs [2] (fig. 23d, k [8, 9]).

Rings were attached to goods line arms; these rings were painted white on the working face, and black on the back of the arm (sometimes limited to that part of the ring which was visible above and below the arm) [2]. On ringed arms, the front and back straight stripes were replaced by circular dots [2] although this may not have been done originally [10]. Later, in S R days, the fronts of the rings were sometimes painted black instead of white [2] (fig. 23.1 [5]).

In certain cases, more particularly in the London area, the white stripes on the front of arms were replaced by lettering or numbers to indicate the routes or roads to which the signals applied [2, 7].

The posts were white in the case of single -post and bracket signals, but lattice gantries were regarded as part of the "footings" of posts and were therefore black, the individual dolls being painted white [2].

Finials were normally white, but on occasions the ball or the cruciform part was finished in red [11]—probably a local variation only [12] (fig. 23a [13]).

The ironwork on signals—balance levers, cranks, pulleys, down-rods, lamp casings, spectacle castings, front Annett's shields, back blinders, ladders, etc., were very dark grey (at any rate from late Victorian times) [2]. From about 1936 light grey was adopted unofficially, and the ironwork of many signals was so painted [2] and officially confirmed later [8, 9, 14, 15].

7.3 Subsidiary signals.

There were various types of arms used for different purposes (e.g. the wrongroad arm shown in fig. 23f [5] but the method of painting remained uniform with semaphore running signals [2]. The Southern Railway introduced a standard arm for such signals, painted white with red lines along the top and bottom edges [2], the back of the arm being black and white (fig. 23p [8]).

7.4 Ground signals.

In L S W R days these were normally of the Stevens "drop flap" type. Painting was uniform with running signals, except that the targets were plain red without any white markings [2].

The posts of elevated ground signals were officially white, like other posts, but a short lattice post on No. 2 platform at Basingstoke showed clear signs of having been painted pinkish buff [16]. (Light orange, colour A of Section 6.2). S R practice was to use white [13].

7.5 Colour-light signals.

The basic colour has been gray [14], with matt black display shields and hoods [14].

References

1. Rapier, R. C., "Fixed Signals on Railways" in *Proc. Inst. C.E.,* v. 38 (Session 1873-4, pt. 2), p. 146.
2. Howard Turner, J. T., private communication of notes from his records.
3. Edwards, W. E., in *Railway Magazine,* v. 14, p. 301 (Apr. 1904).
4. Models of these types of signals illustrated in Simmons, T. M., *Railways to the end of the Nineteenth Century,* London, HMSO, 1964, pl. 10.
5. From examination of photographs.
6. Photograph in Kichenside, G. M. and Williams, A , *British Railway Signalling,* London, Ian Allan, 1963, pp. 74-5.
7. Photograph in *Railway and Travel Monthly,* no. 31, p. 401 (Nov. 1912).
8. BR-SR Rules instructional chart no. 2 (revised 1949). Colours defined by ref. 14.
9. BR-SR Rules instructional chart no. 3 (revised 1949). Colours defined by ref. 14.
10. Photograph in *Railway and Travel Monthly,* no. 29, p. 205 (Sept. 1912).
11. Hambleton, F. C., "London and South Western Railway Signals" in *HMRS Journal,* v. 5, pp. 80-2 (1966).
12. Howard Turner, J. T., private communication of opinion.
13. After Hambleton, loc. cit.
14. BR-SR CCE Information Sheet BR(s)E/1/etc. (Dec. 1949, reissued as S.02.17.01, etc. in Jan. 1960).
15. This was associated with the introduction of colour-light signals (private communication from Mr. G. H. Platt).
16. Writer's observations, 1965.

Section 8 Road Vehicles

8.1 L S W R liveries.

Information has been very hard to come by, and the majority of it has come from the horse-carrying ambulance preserved in the Museum of British Transport.

Close examination of the horse ambulance showed that it had formerly been painted dark green. This paint was perhaps applied in c. 1900.

Colours:

Moderate olive green	7·5 GY 4/4 [1] to
Grayish olive green	7·5 GY 3/2 [1]

It has been strongly urged on the writer that this may have been the Adams dark green of Section 2.6 [2].

8.2 The last painting by the L S W R was, however, in brown and buff presumably derived from the passenger coach livery.

Colours:

A:	Dark grayish reddish brown	2·5 YR 2/2 est. [1]
B:	Moderate orange yellow	7·5 YR 8/8 [1]
C:	Red	
D:	Gray	

The body was dark brown, with the company's name in full in dark brown on a buff band running the length of the body. The wheels were red, as were the axles and swivelling carriage, and the interior of the driver's area was gray. Small lettering was white [1]. Similar colouring applied to the rail-carried road (horse) vans for meat traffic [3]. What appears to be an official specification for road vehicle painting [4, 5] ran:

> On body—two coats lead colour, one coat solid brown, one coat varnish. On fascia—three coats solid brown, one coat varnish colour, two coats finishing varnish, lettering as required.
>
> On wheels and under-carriage—two coats light Venetian, one coat oil red, one coat varnish and red, and two coats of varnish.

Plate 8a, taken in 1903, shows a local carrier's van of indeterminate dark colouring with an L S W R tilt. Platform trolleys were very dark brown, with white lettering [6, 7].

8.3 The colouring of the early L S W R motor omnibuses used in Devon has not been found recorded. Probably the saloons were varnished around the windows with dark brown lower parts. The initials L S W R on the sides were probably gilt —there were two forms, block letters [8] and ornate initials [9].

8.4 Southern Railway vehicles.

Colours:

A: Green [10]

B: Chinese red [10]

The exterior of body, including ironwork to be painted green with wheels, forecarriage, shafts (or pole) and undergear Chinese red. The interior of the body to be painted green except the floor which was to be painted lead colour. The tail-board was to be painted green both sides, the underside of the driver's footrest to be Chinese red. All chains and ironwork on the shafts and poles to be black [10].

The railway's name was to be painted in yellow block letters, 3¼ in. and 2½ in. high (plate 7e) on both sides with Company Secretary's name (e.g. GODFREY KNIGHT WATERLOO STN LONDON) in white 1¼ in. letters on the off side only. The tare weight and distributed load (e.g. 4 TONS) were to be in 1 in. yellow letters on both sides, and the vehicle number in 3¼ in. yellow figures in the centre of the front board of the body and on the off side only. The painting date (e.g. 2-23) was to be marked on the off side only, low down near the tail-board, and the vehicle number (e.g. S R 1401) to be incised in the off-side shaft in two-inch letters [10]. Plate 7e seems to show the letters S R on the van tilt; this was certainly the regular practice [11].

8.5 Motor vehicles.

The colouring of motor vehicles belonging to both the L S W R and S R followed the precedents set for horse-drawn carts. In the 1920s the full company name was marked on the cab side behind the driver's door [12] and along the side rails of trailers. SOUTHERN or SOUTHERN RAILWAY was also often marked on the cab front above the windscreen [10].

8.6 Revised lettering.

From the 1930s onwards, white, outlined lettering of Gill Sans derivation (see Section 6.9) was used, and continued in use until nationalisation together with the basic colour scheme described above [13].

References

1. Observations by the writer, 1964.
2. Howard Turner, J. T., private communication of opinion.
3. Photograph in *Railway Magazine*, v. 28, p. 494 (June 1911).
4. Warner, S., in Macaulay, J. (ed.), *Modern Railway Working*, London, Gresham Publishing Co., 1912.
5. Warner, S., in Bell, A. R. et al. (eds.), *Railway Mechanical Engineering*, London, Gresham Publishing Co., 1923, v. 1, p. 184.
6 Ellis, C. H., private communication of recollections.
7. Howard Turner, J. T., private communication of contemporary notes.
8. Photograph in Ellis, C. H., *The South Western Railway*, London, George Allen and Unwin, 1956, betw. pp. 176-7. Shown in colour (perhaps imaginatively) in Crosville Motor Services Ltd. calendar (March) 1968. (Copy in HMRS archives).
9. Photograph in *Railway Magazine*, v. 31, p. 9 (July 1912).

Section 9 Miscellaneous items of livery

9.1 Coach destination boards

The L S W R pattern of these seems to have been standardised by about 1890 and because of the need for interchangeability the same size was used right through to nationalisation. Wooden boards 2 ft. 7 in. x 3½ in. x ½ in. [1] were fitted into pairs of brackets just below the cant-rail [2]. The usual colouring was red with white block lettering [3, 4], sometimes with black shading [4], but those for the ocean liner trains running to Southampton were blue with white letters [4] and some boards were pinkish, probably the carriage salmon colour, with gilt letters shaded in black [4].

Larger boards were fitted to the roofs of dining saloons and these were red with white letters shaded black [4]. From 1921 onwards this sort of board was used on ordinary coaches in important trains, the colouring being that of contemporary coaches, i.e. green with gilt Roman letters outlined in black [4, 5], and this style was perpetuated by the Southern Railway [4]. The paired small brackets were utilised by the S R to carry coach identity boards — elongated octagonal boards with a bold letter on them to facilitate seat-finding [2] — as well as to carry destination boards on suburban services. The latter boards were white with green letters for steam services and with red letters for electric routes [6]. For quick changes, pasted-on paper labels were used from 1929 onwards; these were plain black on white [4].

9.2 Uniforms.

It would not be right to end a book about liveries without acknowledging the main meaning of the word. Between the report of the uniforms worn by L S R guards in 1840 (scarlet coats with silver buttons and lace collars; bright blue trousers with two rows of scarlet piping [7] — later, c. 1844, perhaps modified to brown tail coats with pale blue trousers [8] (outfits perhaps designed to attract the reliable ex-servicemen who were sought after by the early railways as their best source of disciplined employees) — and the note that red neckties were introduced by Minute of the Board in 1893 [9] as a useful emergency signal, there is little which a non-specialist can record, except to note that B R seem to have been reading the Minute books in recent years too. The general run of working clothes appears in some of the Plates in this book and the basic outfit of jean jacket and trousers is common to most enginemen; station staff had degrees of formality of uniform, culminating in the *gold hat* of a stationmaster [10]. It has been suggested to me [11] that the lady in Plate 6a is in fact in uniform — the date of the photograph is quite likely to be around 1915-20 and photographs show the wartime ticket collectors at Waterloo to have had issue dresses with L S W R embroidered on them [12].

9.3 Ships' flags.

Both the L S W R and the S R had house flags for their cross-channel ships, and these are shown below in figs. 24 and 25 [2] respectively. The L S W R flag was blue with a version of the Company's arms on it [13].

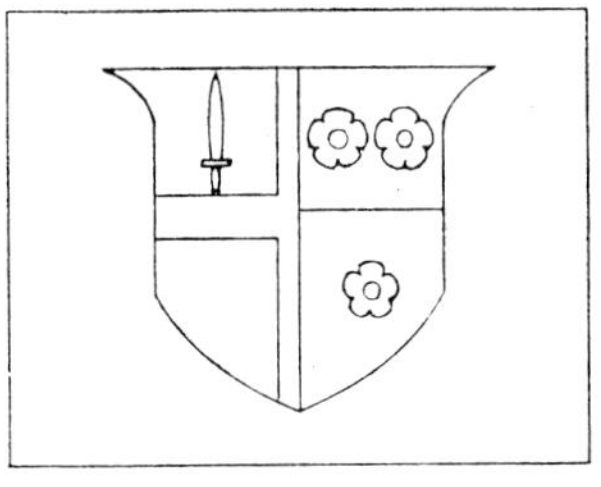

Fig. 24

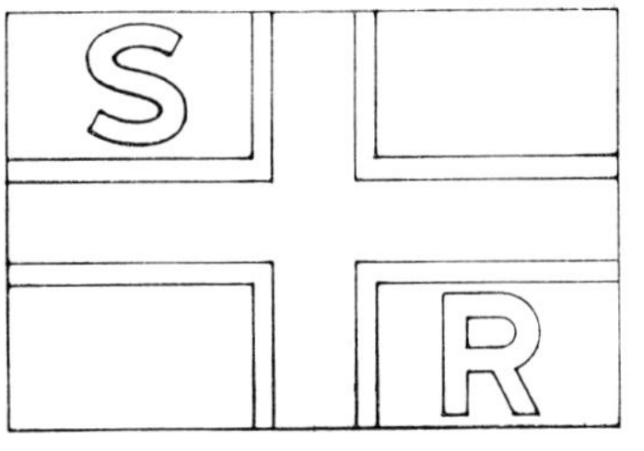

Fig. 25

References

1. Bishop, M., private communication quoting details of board from the Lynton and Barnstaple Railway, in the Narrow Gauge Railway Museum, Towyn. These boards are believed to have been introduced to the line by the L S W R in 1922.
2. From photographs.
3. Ellis, C. H., *The South Western Railway*, London, George Allen and Unwin, 1956, p. 29.
4. Howard Turner, J. T., private communication.
5. Photograph in *South Western Gazette* (July 1922).
6. Tumilty, H. V., private communication.
7. *Railway Magazine*, location not known.
8. Cunnington, P., *Occupational Costume in England*, London, Adam and Charles Black, 1967, p. 222.
9. *Ibid.*, p. 220.
10. *Railway and Travel Monthly*, v. 5 (Sept. 1912).
11. I am grateful to Mrs. Janet Woolgar for this idea.
12. Although a novelist describes all the staff then as being trousered — Williams, H., *A Test to Destruction*, London, Macdonald, 1960, p. 114.
13. From a model of P. S. *Wolf* (owned by the L S W R 1871-1902) in the Tudor House Museum, Southampton.

A1.1 The study of L S W R liveries is at once helped and confused by the existence of a number of recipes for the preparation of batches of paint from the raw ingredients. While there seems no reason to doubt their authenticity, it is not possible to be sure of the dating of these recipes and so uncertainty remains as to what stage they represent in the development of the liveries. The existence of more than one recipe for a given colour also raises the possibility that other colours may have been composed in different ways from those given below. How far this was so is also uncertain and the colour values quoted in the preceding sections are given to aid judgement of the limits between which given nominal colours have been found to vary.

A1.2 Torbay red oxide

This paint was probably based on iron oxide worked at Brixham, Devon. The main constituent was the same as that used as the basis of Venetian and Indian reds[1].

A1.3 Engine green [2, 3, 4] (alias royal green and tartan green)

Cypress green (colour no. 277 of BS 381C:1948)	4 lb.
Zinc white in oil	2 lb.
Lemon chrome in oil	1 lb.

In considering this colour, the best starting point is the information that it was known as "royal green". This term refers to a range of deep Brunswick greens [5], that is, green pigments produced by mixing Chinese blue — which is a form of Prussian blue — with lemon chrome in the very rough proportions of 1:5 (for a light shade). This mixture constitutes royal green in itself[6], but the L S W R formula adds a further 1½ units of lemon chrome and 3 units of zinc white. The choice of zinc white is confirmation that the Cypress green involved a Brunswick green pigment. The addition of zinc white to a paint is recommended to reduce pitting corrosion under the paint film and to improve brushing qualities[7].

It is not certain whether Drummond's green was originally the same as Adam's, but it seems likely that the lemon chrome ingredient represents an addition to the original formula (note the statements in section 2.9 that the colour became more yellowish in the early years of the twentieth century). It is tempting to speculate that Drummond had developed a bias against blue paints during his service with the Caledonian Railway — Mr. D. Burton points out that he was often told that it was difficult to maintain the blue colouring on the boilers of C R locomotives, for it tended to darken with heat[8]. It might be that Drummond, having had his yellow livery rejected, elected to reduce gradually the proportion of blue pigment in the L S W R paint.

An alternative suggestion is that the gradual yellowing of the Drummond green may have been due to the use of different, possibly cheaper grades of lead chrome, which varies from primrose through orange to scarlet [9]. The fact that costs of painting engines were carefully calculated in 1909 [10] may be an indication that the motive for the change was an economic one.

The changeover to sage green in the early months of the 1914-18 war may also be of more significance than has previously been noted. No known L S W R formulation for this paint survives, but two sources, one of them certainly contemporary, give recipes for colours of this name, viz.:

Sage green [11]

White lead	1 part
Chrome green	4 parts
Ivory black	1 part

(Chrome green to be made from Prussian blue (1 part) and light chrome yellow (8 parts).

Sage green [11] (alternative to that above)

White lead
French ochre
Lamp black
Prussian blue
— the proportions are not specified.

Sage green [12]

White lead	100 parts
Medium chrome green	3 parts
Raw umber	1 part

While these recipes may give widely differing colours, it seems fairly certain that the L S W R sage green will have been a greyish shade, and it is at least possible that the object of the change may have been to reduce the chrome content of the paint. The significance of this is that chrome greens are produced, as noted above, from lemon chrome [13], and that pigment is made by a process of which the starting point is lead nitrate, a chemical important in the manufacture of explosives [14].

To account for the reports of a "sickly green", or olive, colour in conjunction with the simplified painting introduced by Urie in 1917, it may be recalled that that was the year of the intensive German submarine blockade of western Europe, when the home market was deliberately deprived of any imports which could be done without. While there is, again, no direct evidence, it seems likely that a recipe such as the following may have been employed:

Olive green [15]

French (yellow) ochre	70%
Raw umber	30%

— the pigments of which can be obtained from home sources.

A1.4 The name **tartan green** is, in contrast, associated with a very dark shade of green. The British Colour Council currently lists it as an alternative name for Lincoln green[16], CC 108, which has an approximate Munsell reference of 5 G 2/4 est. and is hardly distinguishable from Deep Brunswick Green, colour no. 227 of BS 381C:1964 (10 GY 2/4). Since the B C C Dictionary was compiled from a consensus of what colour-using trades meant by given colour names, it is possible that "tartan green' was in fact the dark goods green of which so little has been written.

A1.5 **Purple brown** [2, 3, 4]
Purple brown in oil 6 lb.
Burnt sienna in oil 4 oz.
Burnt umber in oil 4 oz.

The pigment purple brown (oxide of iron) is today prepared in accordance with BS 3981:1966, but this specification does not define a colour standard. The B C C standard is CC 186, which is similar to Light Purple Brown, colour no. 449 of BS 381C:1964 (approx. Munsell ref. 7.5 R 2/4). Purple brown oxide paint is recommended for the coating of steelwork, and one may speculate that the reason Drummond specified the brown edging to his panels was to give extra protection at the most vulnerable places and thereby extend the life of the paint job, but it should be noted that the pigment itself was not developed until 1905. The unofficial name "cardinal red" also features in the B C C list as Cardinal, CC 16, of which the approximate Munsell reference is dark red, 5 R 3/7.

A1.6 **Dark brown** [2, 3, 4]
Quaker green in oil 2 lb. 2 oz.
Purple brown in oil 6 oz.
Orange chrome yellow ½ oz.
Drop black in oil ½ oz.

The term "Quaker green" seems to have been in widespread use in the nineteenth century. It is on one showing the name of a class of Brunswick greens [17], but was also used as name for a domestic paint of a lighter shade [18]. However, the *New English Dictionary* lists "Quaker colour" as a drab or grey colour and cites it as used as a synonym for snuff colour in 1818. The speculation that the quakerishness consisted in the dullness of the colour seems very reasonable, but the term cannot be taken to have a precise meaning.

While this book was in proof, a list of constituents (but not proportions) for **Quaker green** has been found [19]:
Venetian red
Chrome yellow
Blue black
(Blue black to be made from drop black (19 parts) and Prussian blue (1 part).)

A1.7 **Body brown** [20, 21]
Quaker green } powder 28 lb.
Purple brown } powder 5 lb. 4 oz.
Orange chrome } powder 8 oz.
To be ground in linseed oil as for Salmon brown. Two coats; varnish in second coat.

This recipe is repeated, with the exception that the quantity of Quaker green is given as 26 lb., in [22].

A1.8 **Lining brown** [20]
Quaker green 6 lb.
Purple brown 1 lb. 4 oz.
Orange chrome 2 oz.
Ground in linseed oil. After painting, three coats of varnish flatting down between coats.

A1.9 **Salmon pink** [2, 4]
White lead in oil 4 lb. 5 oz.
Burnt sienna in oil 3 oz.
Venetian red in oil 2½ oz.
Middle chrome yellow in oil ¾ oz.

Attempts to reconstitute "salmon" from the L S W R recipes tend to produce shades which are noticeably darker and more red than the surviving specimens. It may be that fading is to blame for this, but since most of the specimens have been examined after the removal of surface layers this does not seem likely; in any case the pigments concerned are of good permanency. The explanation is probably that modern pigments have greater staining power than the older ones.

The British Colour Council lists Salmon Buff as an eighteenth century colour name [16], and give it the designation CC 43 (approximate Munsell reference 2·5 YR 8/5 est.) Salmon Pink is listed as CC 38 (approximate Munsell reference 10 R 6/9 est.).

The L S W R recipe differs from both British and U.S.A. versions of 'salmon', which are based on chrome pigments in white lead, viz.:

Salmon [11]
White lead 6 parts
Vermilion 1 part
Chrome yellow (pale) —
or
(White lead presumed)
Raw sienna
Burnt sienna
Burnt umber
and
Salmon [23]
White lead 50 parts
Deep orange chrome 5 parts

In view of the known dates of some of the L S W R compositions, it seems likely that those printed in Appendices A1.9, 10, 11, 12 are all wartime substitutes for a now lost pre-war formula.

A1.10 **Salmon pink** [3, 24]
As A1.9 but calls for 1½ oz. of Venetian red in lieu of 2½ oz. It is possible that this represents a recent transcription error of the above recipe.

A1.11 **Salmon brown** [20]
White lead 2½ cwt.
Burnt sienna 12 lb.
Venetian red 10 lb.
Mid chrome (yellow) 3½ lb.

To be ground in linseed oil. Then thin down with turps and a little sun driers ready for use. Two coats of this with varnish added to the second coat.

A1.12 **Salmon brown** [21]
As A1.11 but calls for 10½ lb. of Venetian red in lieu of 10 lb. The A1.12 recipe, but with

the quantities doubled, has been noted in Eastleigh records [22].

A1.13 Lining red [20]
Light vermilion red (dry) ground in linseed oil.

A1.14 S R olive green [25]

Yellow ochre	%
Prussian blue	%

"The ochre was inclined to dissolve and give way to the Prussian in a thoroughly yellow manner."

A1.15 Malachite green
This name refers to a pigment which is derived from coal tar, as well as to the mineral of that name. It is listed as colour no. CC 94 of the BCC [16] and has an approximate Munsell reference of 10 GY 4/5. Mr. J. T. Howard Turner has supplied the following note on the paint used by the S R: "It was, I was told at the time, produced by adding yellow and blue to the *Brilliant green* used for ironwork on stations etc. Under weathering, it assumed a rather bluer tint than when new. Hence variations were soon apparent. After the war a somewhat darker shade was used — produced, I understand, by adding a little black to the previous mix. Even when darker, however, it was much lighter than the present (1970) B R - S R rolling stock green. The darker version also weathered to a more bluish tone, so that variations were legion. This bluish tint could also be seen on station ironwork, so that it must have come from decomposition of the green rather than from any other source." [26]

A1.16 Coach umber [27]

Raw umber	50%
Burnt umber	50%

A1.17 Standard brown for wagons (Ashford works) [28].

Burnt umber	70 lb.
Raw umber	56 lb.

Umber, zinc oxide and Japan to be obtained from Messrs. Denton and Jutsum or other approved makers.

A1.18 Pinkish buff [29]

Stone ochre	5 lb.
White lead	4 oz.
Lemon chrome	2 oz.
Burnt sienna	1 oz.

Driers and linseed oil to make up 7 lb.

A1.19 Pale stone [29]

White lead	5 lb.
Stone ochre	4 oz.
Raw sienna	2 oz.

Driers and linseed oil to make up 7 lb.

A1.20 Dark brown [29]

Burnt sienna	5 lb.
Burnt Turkey umber	5 oz.

Driers and linseed oil to make up 7 lb.

A1.21 Experimental reconstruction of 'Salmon'.
A mixture of modern artists' oil colours prepared in the L S W R proportions (Appendix 1.10) gave a colour of grayish red, 7·5 R 5/6. A sample of this paint was allowed to dry and placed in the open on a south-facing window-cill. After exposure for twelve months the colour had faded to dark yellowish pink, 7·5 R 6/6 est. I am grateful to Mr C. J. Peacock for making this test and lending me the specimens. Mr P. E. Barnes kindly sent me a specimen of 'salmon' which he had used on models and found accepted by people who recalled the L S W R colour. This shade was grayish reddish orange, 2·5 YR 5/6 est.

References

1. Remington, J. S., and Dr. W. Francis, *Pigments, their Manufacture, Properties and Use,* London, Leonard Hill, 3rd edn. revised 1954, p. 138.
2. B R-S R records, Eastleigh works, undated notes obtained by A. B. Macleod in 1948 (attributed by him to c.1903).
3. Maskelyne, J. N., in *Model Railway News*, v. 24, p. 203 (Nov. 1948).
4. Carter, E. F., *Britain's Railway Liveries . . . 1825-1948*, London, Harold Starke, 1963, p. 135.
5. Remington and Francis, op. cit., pp. 121, 122.
6. Ibid, pp. 121, 122, 204.
7. Ibid, pp. 22, 23, 204.
8. Burton, D., private communication quoting conversations with old C R employees at St. Rollox works, Glasgow, c. 1936.
9. Taylor, C. J. A. and Marks, S. (Eds.), *Paint Technology Manuals, pt. 6: Pigments, Dyestuffs and Lakes*, London, Chapman and Hall for the Oil and Colour Chemists' Association, 1966, p. 159.
10. Bradley, D. L., *Locomotives of the London and South Western Railway*, Solihull, Railway Correspondence and Travel Society, pt. 1, 1965, p. 17.
11. Matthews, P., *The Painter's Pocket Book*, London and Manchester, John Heywood, 1905, p. 71.
12. Hiscox, G. D. (Ed.), *Henley's Twentieth Century Book of Formulas, Processes and Trade Secrets,* New York, N.Y., Norman W. Henley Publishing Co., 1907, edn. of 1955, p. 559.
13. Taylor and Marks, op. cit., p. 172.

14. Snell, F. D. and C. T., *Dictionary of Commercial Chemicals*, Princeton, N. J., D. van Nostrand, 1962, p. 173.
15. Minrath, W. R. (Ed.), *Van Nostrand's Practical Formulary*, Princeton, N. J., D. van Nostrand, 1957, p. 64.
16. *Dictionary of colours for interior decoration,* London, British Colour Council, 1949, v. 3. This was based on a pre-war survey of then currently accepted meanings for colour names.
17. Remington, J. S., *The Paint Laboratory Note Book*, London, Leonard Hill, 3rd edn. 1946, p. 59.
18. Hughes, W. J., private communication. See also *Model Engineer,* v. 133 pp. 872-3 (6 Sept. 1968).
19. Matthews, op. cit., pp. 70, 64.
20. B R-S R information. This recipe is associated with the date Sept. 1915.
21. B R-S R under reference "per C & W Engineer,, Eastleigh, CW 90/27, C/Y 9 Sept. 1955".
22. BR-SR records, Eastleigh works, letter under reference CW 90/27 from Eastleigh drawing office to PR&PO Waterloo in reply to letter of Nov. 1954.
23. Hiscox, op. cit., p. 558.
24. Peacock, C. J., in *South Western Circular*, no. 14, pp. 95-9 (Winter 1968).
25. Day-Lewis, S., *Bulleid, Last Giant of Steam,* London, George Allen and Unwin, 1964, p. 231.
26. Howard Turner, J. T., private communication.
27. 'Sparks' (Maj.—Sparkes) in *Model Railway News* v. 5, p. 340 (Nov. 1929).
28. BR-SR records, Eastleigh works. Information from Mr. R. Chorley.
29. L S W R, *Specification for the painting of station name-boards*, Engineer's office, Waterloo, March 1906. Previously quoted by George Dow in *HMRS Journal*, v. 2, pp. 25, 27 (1956).

Appendix 2 — Paint fragments

This Appendix lists colours visible in chips of paint collected in 1964-9 by C. J. Peacock, H. V. Tumilty and the writer. The earliest layer is listed first, and unless otherwise stated, all layers present are listed in order. The notes after the Munsell colour references are the writer's interpretation of the visible colour. The original paint fragments are held in the H M R S Library under reference 292.

A2.1 Saloon portion of L S W R inspection locomotive no. 733, built 1899, renumbered 058S Dec. 1924, repainted by S R Feb. 1932.

A2.1.1 Right side, body panel below waist-line.

Reddish brown	2·5 YR 5/5—Filler (3 coats)
Black	—
Moderate yellow green	5 GY 5/6—L S W R loco. green
Dark brown	2·5 YR 2/2 est.—Body brown
Moderate olive green	5 GY 4/6—S R coach green

Black, silver and dark yellowish green (2·5 G 3/3) domestic paints.

A2.1.2 Right side, panel immediately below vent hood.

Yellowish white	2·5 Y 8/4
Dark brown	2·5 YR 3/2 est.—Filler (thick)
Moderate olive green	7·5 GY 4/3 L S W R loco. green
Brownish orange	5 YR 5/8—Salmon
Strong orange	5 YR 6/11—Salmon (2 or more coats)
Black	—(thick)
Medium gray	10 B 5/0·5 est.
Very light green	7·5 G 8/6—domestic paint.

A2.1.3 Left side, moulding, and

A2.1.4 Right side, rear corner pillar below waist-line.

Light yellowish pink	7·5 R 9/3—primer
Dark brown	5 YR 1·5/4 est.
Black	—
Moderate yellow green	5 GY 5/6—L S W R loco. green
Dark brown	2·5 YR 2/2 est.
Gilt with $\frac{1}{8}$ in. red stripe	7·5 R 4/11—curve of moulding
Moderate olive green	7·5 GY 4/4—S R coach green

Gray, black and green domestic paints.

A2.1.5 Panel above waist-line.

Moderate brown	5 YR 4/3 est.—filler
Moderate yellow green	5 GY 5/6—L S W R loco. green
Light orange	5 YR 8/7—Salmon
Black	—(thick)

A2.1.6 Droplight frame

Reddish brown	7·5 R 4/6 est.—"Mahogany" (several coats)
Grayish olive green	5 GY 3/2
Black	—(thick)

A2.2 Body of L S W R 19 ft. 11 in. third class coach, c. 1865, number not known, grounded at Bournemouth West. The body had long since been tarred over and this had sealed the earlier coats of paint.

A2.2.1 Door pillar above waist.

Pink	5 YR 9/3—primer
Light gray	N 8—undercoat
Moderate brown	7·5 YR 4/5—"teak"
Moderate Orange	2·5 YR 7/6—Salmon (3 coats)
Brownish gray	—too small to match
Moderate reddish brown	7·5 R 3/4—engineers' colour?
Tar	—

The colour of the angle of the moulding was not distinguishable from that of the lower panels of the body.

A2.2.2 Door pillar below waist.

Pink	5 YR 9/3—primer
Light gray	N 8—undercoat
Moderate brown	7·5 YR 4/5—"teak"
Brownish gray	10 YR 3/1—Body brown
Brownish gray	2·5 Y 3/1—Body brown (in second sample)

The last two shades can hardly be distinguished from black except in bright sunlight.

A2.2.3 Interior of end, approx. 5 ft. above floor.

Pale orange yellow	7·5 YR 9/4 } 4 coats each, alternately.
Varnish	— }
White	— } 2 coats each, alternately.
Varnish	— }
Moderate yellowish pink	2·5 YR 8/4—Stone

n.b. ceiling paint continuously white.

A2.2.4 External moulding on end at corner, approx 5 ft. above floor.

Pink	—too small to match
Strong brown	5 YR 4/6—"teak"
Moderate yellowish pink	10 R 8/4—Salmon?
Strong yellowish brown	7·5 YR 5/6—Salmon
Tar	—

See A2.5 for hypothesis that interior repaints were at 4-year intervals. On this basis, white interiors introduced c. 1882 and last interior repaint c. 1890. Since there are 4 coats of exterior finish present, compared with 7 interior, if the exterior was never stripped it may have been repainted at 8-year intervals, perhaps 1890, 1882, 1874. The latter date might be that of the introduction of "salmon". The confused layering of sample 4 suggests that the moulding was picked out to contrast with the panels.

A2.3 Body of 30 ft. second class coach, c. 1885, grounded at St. Kew Highway about 1914.

Black	—
Gray	N 9
Light yellowish pink	2·5 YR 9/3—Salmon
Moderate reddish brown	2·5 YR 3/3—Lining colour
Light gray	N 8
Moderate yellowish pink	2·5 YR 8/4
Black	—
Light gray	N 8
Moderate yellowish pink	2·5 YR 8/4
Moderate reddish brown	2·5 YR 3/3
Moderate orange	2·5 YR 7/6
Dark grayish brown	5 YR 2/2
Moderate orange	2·5 YR 7/6

A2.4 Body of 30 ft. third class coach, grounded at Holsworthy; paint taken from hollow of cant-rail moulding.

Black	—
Moderate yellowish pink	5 YR 8/4 } 2 coats each, alternately.
Varnish	— }
Moderate yellowish pink	2·5 YR 7/5 } 3 coats each, alternately.
Varnish	— }
Moderate yellowish pink	2·5 YR 7/5
Dark grayish brown	5 YR 2/2

A2.5 Body of 30 ft. "birdcage" passenger brake van, c. 1885, grounded at Bournemouth West. Number not known.

A2.5.1 Interior of side, approx. 5 ft. above floor.

Strong yellowish brown	—
White	7·5 YR 5/6
Varnish (or black)	—
Pale orange yellow	7·5 YR 8·5/4—3 coats
Moderate orange	5 YR 6/6—2 coats
Black	—not tar

A2.5.2 End, moulding near cant-rail.

Pale yellow	5 Y 9/3
Gray	N 9—undercoat
Moderate orange yellow	7·5 YR 7/6
Dark pink	5 R 6/6—ground colour
Vivid red	7·5 R 3·5/16—warning colour
Tar	—

A2.5.3 Luggage door, waist panel.

Light gray	N 8—primer
Grayish red	5 R 5/2—ground colour
Brownish orange	5 YR 5/8—Salmon
Vivid red	5 R 5/13—lining?
Gilt	—lettering?
Tar	—

Interior painted white once, say in 1885. A2.2.3 shows final internal repaint also in white and probably about the same time. Thus the 1865 coach has 5 more coats of paint than the brake van and is 20 years older. This suggests that internal repainting was done at 4-year intervals. If this is true then the brown internal finish was probably introduced c. 1890 and the brake van was last repainted c. 1910. The ceiling was continuously white.

A2.6 24 ft. milk van built 1919 as L S W R no. 5011, renumbered S R no. 1437 on 6th Dec. 1924 and 1687S in Nov. 1940, serving as battery charging van no. DS 1687 in May, 1966.

A2.6.1 Side louvres, approx. 12 in. above floor.

Moderate yellowish pink	7·5 R 7/4—primer
Light gray	N 8—undercoat
Grayish olive green	5 GY 3/2—2 coats, discolouring to
Olive gray	2·5 GY 3/1—L S W R sage green
Medium gray	N 6—undercoat
Dark yellowish green	2·5 GY 3/3—2 coats, S R green
Bluish gray	10 B 5·5/1—undercoat
Dark yellowish green	2·5 G 4/6—Malachite green

A2.6.2 End.

Moderate yellowish pink	7.5 R 8/3—primer
Dark grayish reddish brown	2.5 YR 2/2—L S W R body brown?
Black	—?
Grayish olive green	5 GY 3/2—L S W R sage green
Black	—S R colour
Medium gray	N 6 } 2 coats each,
Black	— } alternately.

A2.6.3 Flitch-plate of solebar.

Rust	—
Black	—anti-corrosive paint
Grayish brown	5 YR 3/2—filler
Gray	—undercoat
Dark grayish brown	5 YR 2/2 est.—L S W R body brown
Moderate olive green	5 GY 4/3—L S W R sage green
Black	—S R underframe colour (more than 4 coats)

A2.7 24 ft. milk van built 1910 as L S W R no. 6, renumbered 5006 in Feb. 1918, S R no. 1432 on 25th July 1925 and no. 993S on 12th Dec. 1935, withdrawn 13th July 1946, sold and grounded at Wickham, Hants.

A2.7.1 Moulding near cant-rail.

Moderate olive green	5 GY 4/6—L S W R sage green
Gray	N 9—undercoat
Moderate olive green	5 GY 4/6—early S R green
Pale yellow	4 Y 8/5—perhaps faded from
Black and strong yellow	2·5 Y 7/10 est.—lining
Grey	N 9—undercoat
Dark grayish green	10 GY 3/2—S R green, 1935

Two sets only of S R transfers (gilt and black) were detected, so the first coat of paint is assumed to have been put on by the L S W R.

A2.8 44 ft. bogie specie van built 1913 as L S W R no. 5350, renumbered S R no. 1689 on 26th July 1924 and BR DS 109 on 10th Sept. 1949, panel on sliding door.

Moderate olive green	5 GY 3/3 est.—early S R green
Dark green	7·5 G 3/6—Malachite green
Light gray	N 8
Strong yellow green	7·5 GY 5/7
Dark yellowish green	2·5 G 4/4—discolouring to
Dark yellowish green	2·5 G 3/3

A2.9 56 ft. brake third coach built 1910 as L S W R no. 1520, renumbered S R no. 2975 and later BR DS 1119.

A2.9.1 End face of ducket.

Moderate olive green	5 GY 4/3—S R olive green c. 1940
Dark bluish green	10 G 3/5—Malachite green
Black	—
Dark bluish green	10 G 3/5—c. 1949?
Dark brown	5 YR 1·5/4
Medium gray	N 5
Black	—
Grayish red	7·5 R 4/6 est.
Moderate reddish brown	7·5 R 3/6—BR finish

A2.9.2 Side, below mouldings.

Dark bluish green	10 G 3/5—Malchite green
Medium gray	N 6
Strong yellow green	7·5 GY 5/7
Dark yellowish green	10 GY 4/5 est.—discolouring to
Dark yellowish green	2·5 G 3/3—BR coach green

A2.10 4-SUB motor coach built 1925 as S R no. 8143 or 4 (set no. 1293 and later 3147), body.

Moderate olive green	2·5 GY 3/3—2 coats, c. 1938 green?
Moderate green	5 G 5/6 } one application
Strong green	5 G 4/7 } together,
Dark green	7·5 G 3/6 } probably S R
Strong green	5 G 4/7—6 coats, apparently one repaint, BR coach green
Dark yellowish green	2·5 G 3/3—surface appearance

A2.11 18 ft. insulated banana van built after 1914 as L S W R 15035, renumbered S R no. 50488, withdrawn after 1938 (oiling dates marked), sold and grounded at Lower Upham, Hants. Paint taken from area of large S R lettering.

Dark grayish yellowish brown	10 YR 3/2—L S W R wagon brown
White	N9—L S W R lettering
Moderate yellowish pink	2·5 YR 8/5—S R stone*
Strong reddish brown	10 R 3/8—S R lettering* (* 2 coats each, alternately)
Moderate yellowish pink	2·5 YR 8/5—S R stone, discolouring to
Light yellowish brown	10 YR 6·5/5—with 1936 lettering

A2.12 18ft. fruit van, S R no. apparently 42032, grounded at Fair Oak, Hants. Paint taken from area of large S R lettering.

Dark brown (5 YR 1·5/4) to black: ten layers, alternating with white: nine layers (van showed 1936-type lettering). No general change of basic colour over the years detectable.

A2.13 Lattice girder of footbridge no. 5B, Poole station.

(n.b. primer layers omitted from this description.)

Dark reddish brown	7·5 R 2/4
Medium gray	N 5—3 applications
Light gray	N 7—2 applications
Moderate green	2·5 G 4/6—S R
Strong yellowish green	10 GY 5/8—BR

A2.14 Plate girder of footbridge no. 8, Parkstone station.

Deep reddish orange	7·5 R 4/11
Black	—
Moderate reddish brown	7·5 R 3/6
Light gray	N 7
Black	—
Moderate reddish orange	7·5 R 6/9 est.
Light gray	N 8
Black	—
Moderate reddish orange	7·5 R 6/9 est.
Light gray	N 8
Strong yellowish green	5 G 5/7

A2.15 Awning bracket, platform 4, Basingstoke station (part of additions c. 1880).

Black	—
Moderate reddish brown	7·5 R 3/6
Dark bluish gray	10 B 4/0·5
Moderate reddish brown	7·5 R 3/6
Grayish yellow	5 Y 8/2 } 2 coats each,
Very light yellowish green	2·5 G 9/3 } alternately.
Grayish yellow	5 Y 8/2
Moderate brown	5 YR 3/3
Grayish yellow	5 Y 8/2
Very light yellowish green	2·5 G 9/3—undercoat
Brilliant yellowish green	10 GY 8/7—discolouring to
Light olive	10 Y 5/5
Vivid reddish orange	10 R 5/16
Very light yellowish green	2·5 G 9/3 } 2 coats each,
Strong yellow green	7·5 GY 6/7 } alternately.

A2.16 Exterior face of vertical awning plank from Addlestone station.

Yellowish white	5 Y 9·25/1—undercoat
Moderate yellowish pink	2·5 YR 7/4 est.—L S W R stone (2 coats)
Pale yellow	2·5 Y 9/3—undercoat
Light yellowish brown	10 YR 7/5 est.—S R buff
Grayish yellow	5 Y 8/2—undercoat
Moderate orange yellow	7·5 YR 8/6 est.—BR stone

A2.17 Wimbledon Park station, interior wall of booking hall, paint overlaid by L S W R posters dated Oct. 1910 to June 1911, exposed by removal of bookstall c. 1965.

A2.17.1 Wall below moulding at waist height.

Light gray	2·5 Y 8/0·5
Moderate yellowish pink	5 YR 8/4—L S W R stone
Light gray	2·5 Y 8/0·5
Light orange	5 YR 8/8 est.—stone
Light gray	2·5 Y 8/0·5
Light orange	5 YR 8/7
Dark brown	5 YR 1.5/4

A2.17.2 Wall above moulding.

Light gray	2·5 Y 8/0·5
Moderate orange	5 YR 7/6 est.
Light gray	2·5 Y 8/0·5
Light orange	5 YR 8/7
Light gray	2·5 Y 8/0·5
Moderate yellowish pink	2·5 YR 8/4

A2.17 3 Probably from roof structure.

Very pale green	2·5 G 9/2 est.
Light orange	2·5 YR 8/6
Very pale green	2·5 G 9/2 est.
Pale orange yellow	7·5 YR 9/4
Very pale green	2·5 G 9/2 est.
Pale green	2·5 G 6/2

A2.18 Footbridge no. 5A, Poole.

A2.18.1 Wooden framework.

Dark green	7·5 G 3/6—S R green
Light pink	2·5 R 9/3—primer
Moderate orange yellow	7·5 YR 8/7 est., discolouring to
Light yellowish brown	10 YR 6·5/5—BR stone

A.2.18.2 Wooden framework.

Brownish orange	5 YR 5/8—L S W R stone
Grayish yellow	5 Y 7/2
Light brown	5 YR 5/5—L S W R stone
Grayish yellow	5 Y 7/2
Dark yellowish green	10 GY 4/5—S R green
White	—
Moderate orange yellow	7·5 YR 8/6—BR stone

A2.19 Basingstoke station awnings.

A2.19.1 Vertical boarding of platform 2 awning, probably made 1904.

Light yellowish pink	7·5 R 9/3—primer
Moderate orange yellow	10 YR 8/6—L S W R stone
Moderate brown	7·5 YR 4/5—L S W R stone?
Black	—grime?
Light gray	N7—undercoat
Pale brown	—too small to match
Moderate brown	7·5 YR 4/5—L S W R brown
Light gray	N7—undercoat
Moderate brown	7·5 YR 4/5—L S W R brown
Moderate orange yellow	10 YR 8/6—S R stone
Moderate brown	7·5 YR 4/5—?
Light gray	N 7
Light yellow	2·5 Y 9/6—BR stone

A2.19.2 Awning pillar, probably made 1904.

White	—
Moderate brown	7·5 YR 3/4—L S W R brown
Medium gray	N 6
Black	—
Strong reddish orange	10 R 5/12 est.—red lead
Strong yellowish green	2·5 G 5/8—S R/BR green

A2.20 Grove Park station.

Pale yellow	5 Y 9/4 est.
Pale yellow	5 Y 9/2 est.
Moderate orange yellow	7·5 YR 8/8—S R stone

A2.21 Waterloo Junction station.

Light orange yellow	10 YR 9/6
Strong brown	5 YR 4/5—?
Bluish gray	10 B 5·5/1
Dark yellowish green	10 GY 4/5—2 coats, discolouring to
Grayish olive green	5 GY 3/2—S R green

A2.22 Office building, Bricklayers' Arms goods depot.

Moderate reddish brown	7·5 R 3/4—S E C R colour
Black	—
Light gray	N 8 } 2 coats each,
Strong green	5 G 5/8 } alternately

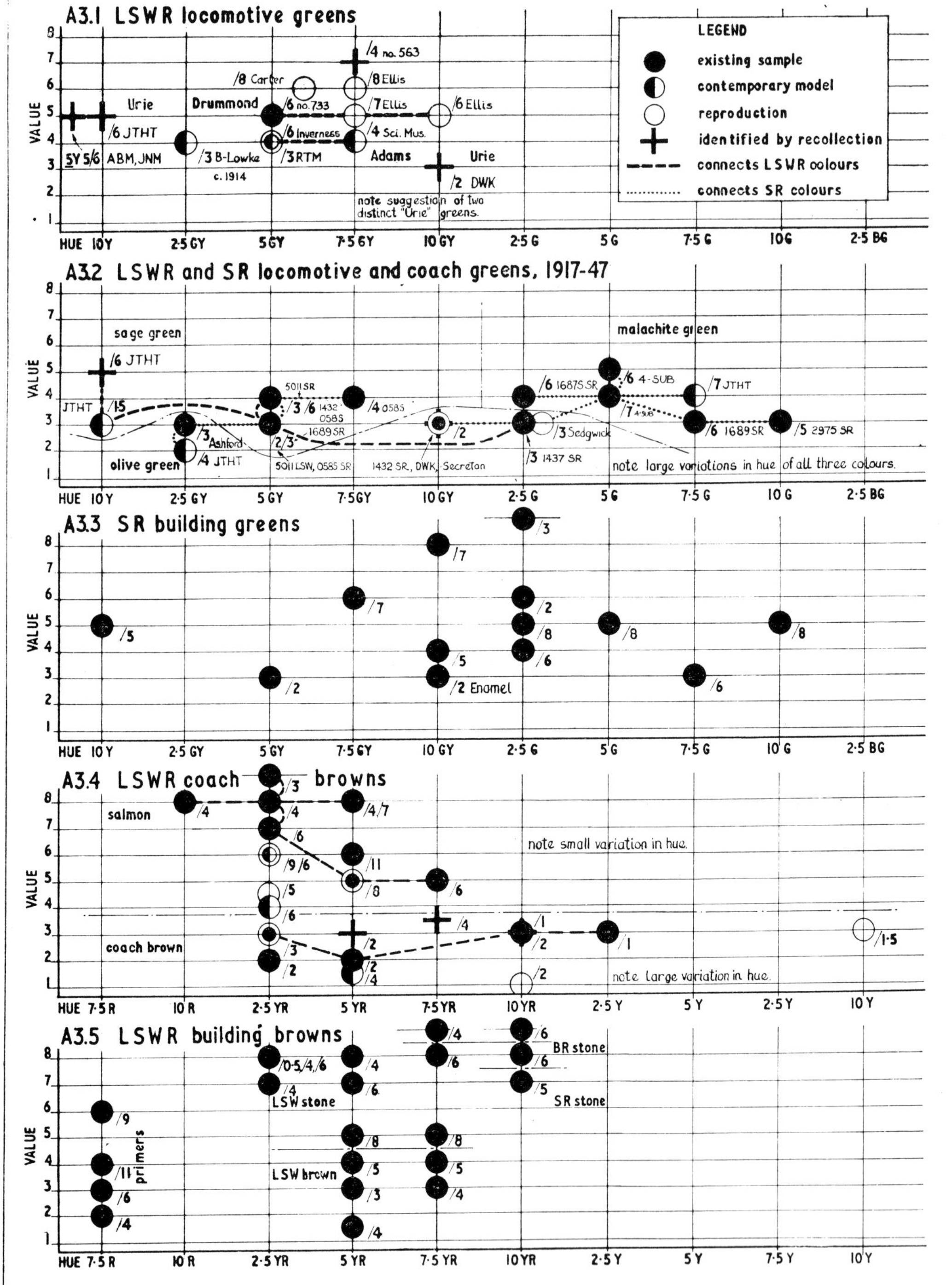
A3.1 LSWR locomotive greens
LEGEND
existing sample
contemporary model
reproduction
identified by recollection
connects LSWR colours
connects SR colours
Urie
Drummond
/6 JTHT
5Y 5/6 ABM, JNM
/3 B-Lowke c. 1914
/8 Carter
/6 no. 733
/6 Inverness
/3 RTM
/4 no. 563
/8 Ellis
/7 Ellis
/4 Sci. Mus.
Adams
/6 Ellis
Urie
/2 DWK
note suggestion of two distinct "Urie" greens.
A3.2 LSWR and SR locomotive and coach greens, 1917-47
sage green
/6 JTHT
JTHT /1.5
olive green
/3 Ashford
/4 JTHT
malachite green
/6 1687S SR
/6 4-SUB
/7 JTHT
/3 Sedgwick
/3 1437 SR
/6 1689SR
/5 2975 SR
note large variations in hue of all three colours.
A3.3 SR building greens
/2 Enamel
A3.4 LSWR coach browns
salmon
coach brown
note small variation in hue.
note large variation in hue.
A3.5 LSWR building browns
LSW stone
LSW brown
primers
BR stone
SR stone
VALUE
HUE

The early stipulation that "every engineman . . . shall always after sunset have a white light on the front of his Engine, and when there is only a single line of rails a Red Light in addition must be placed in front of the Engine, and a Red Light on the side of his Tender; and when travelling without a Train, a Red Light in the rear" [1] was elaborated into a code of white and green lights and white discs arranged differently for the various parts of the Company's system (see table 1). In addition, the beginnings of a whistle code were specified, by which drivers might indicate the route they were due to take at junctions. A passenger train was to carry two red tail lights at night and in fog; if a special train was to follow it, then a red tail board or a third tail light was to be carried. Such a lamp was to be hung from the drawhook, giving a triangle of lights. Goods trains were to have one tail and two side lamps on the last vehicle [2].

The codes of lamps and headboards were elaborated as time went on but few details are available until 1892 when the range of codes listed in Table 2 was promulgated [3]. This was based on the use of four lamp positions. As is confirmed in Section 2.5, the lamp irons were fitted at the top of the smokebox — or for a long while actually on the smokebox door — on either side of the smokebox and at the centre of the buffer beam. Later developments showed an acknowledgement that the situation was getting out of hand, for from 1905 onwards all the varieties of headboard except the plain white disc and diamond were dispensed with in regular service, and to compensate for the reduced number of permutations, the number of lamp-irons was increased to six. The night codes were rationalised in conformity to the simple equations of white disc=white light and white diamond=green light, and by careful attention to geography it was arranged that a dozen or more routes might share the same code without risk of misunderstanding. Further amendments were made in 1911, 1917 (when diamond boards, and more particularly green lights, were dispensed with) and 1921. The official codes of 1905 [4], 1911 [5], 1917 [6] and 1921 [7] are arranged in Table 4.

An unofficial and undated list, compiled by H. C. Clarke [8] has been found to vary slightly from the 1892 code set out in Table 2. The variations are confined to the 17 routes listed in Table 3, while item nos. 21, 22, 23, 25, 48, 49, 57, 60 and 61 of Table 2 are omitted from Clarke's list.

Table 1 Headcodes, 1864

NOTE: Code depends on number not position of discs

	DAY	NIGHT
LONDON AND SOUTHAMPTON	-	W
DIRECT PORTSMOUTH TRAINS	○○	W G
LONDON RICHMOND AND WINDSOR	○	W W
FROM WINDSOR VIA LOOP LINE	-	W
- - - WILLESDEN LINE	○○	W W
KINGSTON AND HAMPTON COURT	○	W W
- - KEW JCT.	○○	W G
BARNES TO HOUNSLOW	-	W
WEYBRIDGE AND CHERTSEY	○	W W
WIMBLEDON AND EPSOM LINE	○	W W
GUILDFORD AND ALTON	○	W W
- - WOKING	-	W G
- - GODALMING	○	W W
WOKINGHAM JCT.	○	W W
BASINGSTOKE AND ANDOVER	○	W W
SALISBURY AND BASINGSTOKE (FISHERTON JCT.)	○	W W
- - BISHOPSTOKE	○○	W G
BISHOPSTOKE AND SALISBURY	-	W
- - PORTSMOUTH	○	W W
FAREHAM AND GOSPORT	-	W
COSHAM JCT.	○	W W
NORTHAM JCT.: FROM BISHOPSTOKE TO DORCHESTER	○	W W
- - - DORCHESTER TO BISHOPSTOKE	○	W W
- - - SOUTHAMPTON TO DORCHESTER	○	W W
- - - DORCHESTER TO SOUTHAMPTON	-	W
DORCHESTER LINE	○	W
POOLE BRANCH	-	W
DORCHESTER AND WEYMOUTH	-	G

When there is only a single line of rails, a Red light in addition must be placed in front of the Engine and a Red light on the side of the Tender.

Table 2 Headcodes, 1892

Bracket positions used: 1 (top), 2 (right), 3 (bottom), 4 (left)

LEGEND: ○ = white disc; ⊕ = white disc with black cross; + = white disc with red cross; ◇ = white diamond; W = white light; G = green light; R = red light

No.	Route	Day 1	Day 2	Day 3	Day 4	Night 1	Night 2	Night 3	Night 4	
1	LONDON AND SOUTHAMPTON VIA BASING						W			
2	- - - WEST (NON STOPPING ONLY)	+				G				
3	- - PORTSMOUTH VIA DIRECT		○		○		W		G	
4	- - EXETER			○				W		
5	WATERLOO LEATHERHEAD GUILDFORD	○	○			W	W			
6	- AND GUILDFORD VIA HAMPTON COURT JCT.		⊕		⊕		W		W	
7	- - HAMPTON COURT	○			○	W			W	
8	- - CHERTSEY VIA VIRGINIA WATER	⊕	⊕			G	G			
9	- - READING		○				W		W	
10	- - WINDSOR	○	◇			W	G			
11	- - LOOP LINES	○	○			W	W			
12	- - KINGSTON ROUNDABOUT	⊕		⊕		G		G		
13	- - - VIA TWICKENHAM					W				
14	- - RICHMOND NEW	+				W		W		
15	- - SHEPPERTON	○			○	W			W	
16	- - NEW WIMBLEDON VIA POINT PLEASANT		○		◇		W		G	
17	- - NINE ELMS	○				G				
18	- - - - ON DOWN WINDSOR LINE	◇		◇		G		W		
19	- - CLAPHAM JCT. (EMPTY TRAINS)	○		○		W		G		
20	- YARD SHUNTING ENGINES	○		○		W		R		
21	NINE ELMS LOCO.- CLAPHAM JCT. (LIGHT ENGINES)	○		○		W		G		
22	CLAPHAM JCT. OR QUEEN'S ROAD TO NINE ELMS LOCO. YARD	◇		○		G		W		
23	- AND KENSINGTON		○		○		W		W	
24	WOKING AND SOUTHAMPTON VIA ALTON	○		○		W		W		
25	- - ASCOT	○				G		W		
26	- - WINDSOR VIA BYFLEET CURVE	○		○		G		G		
27	GUNNERSBURY AND HOUNSLOW	+					W		W	
28	- - TWICKENHAM	⊕			⊕	G			G	
29	LUDGATE HILL AND RICHMOND	○		○		G		G		
30	- - - KINGSTON VIA HAYDON'S ROAD	○				G				
31	- - - - - MERTON ABBEY	◇		○		G		W		
32	GUILDFORD AND ALDERSHOT				○				W	
33	- - GODALMING		○				W		W	
34	FARNHAM AND GUILDFORD	○				W				
35	- - FRIMLEY						W		W	
36	WINCHESTER (DIDCOT RLY.)-SHAWFORD JCT.-SOUTHAMPTON			○	○			W	W	note 1
37	SOUTHAMPTON WEST AND EASTLEIGH	○			○				W	
38	EASTLEIGH AND WEYMOUTH	◇				G				
39	SOUTHAMPTON AND WEYMOUTH	○								
40	- - ANDOVER				○		G		G	
41	- -NORTHAM (LIGHT ENGINES)	◇				G	W			
42	NORTHAM - EASTLEIGH (LIGHT ENGINES)	◇		◇		G		G		
43	SALISBURY AND WIMBORNE	○					W		W	
44	- - SOUTHAMPTON		○		○		W		G	
45	SOUTHAMPTON AND PORTSMOUTH VIA NETLEY	○		○		W		W		
46	EASTLEIGH AND PORTSMOUTH	○					W		W	
47	FAREHAM AND GOSPORT		○		○		W		G	
48	- - STOKES BAY	○				G				
49	BOURNEMOUTH WEST - BROCKENHURST - EASTLEIGH VIA NEW DIRECT	⊕	⊕			G	G			
50	- TURNTABLE	◇				G				
51	YEOVIL BRANCH		○				W		W	
52	CHARD BRANCH		○				W		R	note 2
53	SEATON BRANCH		○				W		R	-
54	SIDMOUTH BRANCH		○				W		R	..
55	EXMOUTH BRANCH		○				W		G	-
56	EXETER AND EXMOUTH JCT. (LIGHT ENGINES)	◇				G				
57	- - PLYMOUTH	○		○		G		G		
58	- - NORTH DEVON		○		○		W		W	
59	HALWILL JCT. AND HOLSWORTHY	◇						G		
60	EXETER OKEHAMPTON AND LAUNCESTON	◇		○		G		W		
61	ILFRACOMBE BRANCH	◇					W		G	note 2

NOTES: 1. On single line, lights to be W R
2. Handing not specified

Table 3 Headcodes of c. 1895

Bracket positions and legend as for table 2.

No.	Route	Day 1	Day 2	Day 3	Day 4	Night 1	Night 2	Night 3	Night 4
2	WATERLOO BOURNEMOUTH AND WEYMOUTH	+				G			
3	" AND PORTSMOUTH VIA WOKING		○		○		W		G
6	" - - - COBHAM		⊕		⊕		W		W
9	" - READING		○		○		W		W
16	" - WIMBLEDON VIA EAST PUTNEY		⊕		◇		W		G
17	" - NINE ELMS (MAIN LINE)	(any position) ⊕				G			
20	" YARD SHUNTING ENGINES	○		○		R		W	
36	WINCHESTER (CHEESEHILL) AND SOUTHAMPTON	○			○	W			W
39	SOUTHAMPTON AND WEYMOUTH					G			
	MIDHURST BRANCH ALSO BRANCHES IN SOUTHERN DISTRICT	○					W		W
	ROYAL TRAIN BETWEEN GOSPORT AND NETLEY	+	○		○	G	W		W
	PILOT TO ABOVE		○	⊕	○		W	G	W
	NINE ELMS AND WEST OF ENGLAND FAST GOODS			○			G	W	G
	WATERLOO AND MERTON ROAD SIDINGS VIA EAST PUTNEY (EMPTY TRAINS)		◇		⊕		G		W
	COSHAM AND HAVANT		◇		○		G		W
	WINDSOR TO KENSINGTON		○		+		?		
	WATERLOO AND ASCOT VIA WOKING	○				G		W	

Table 4

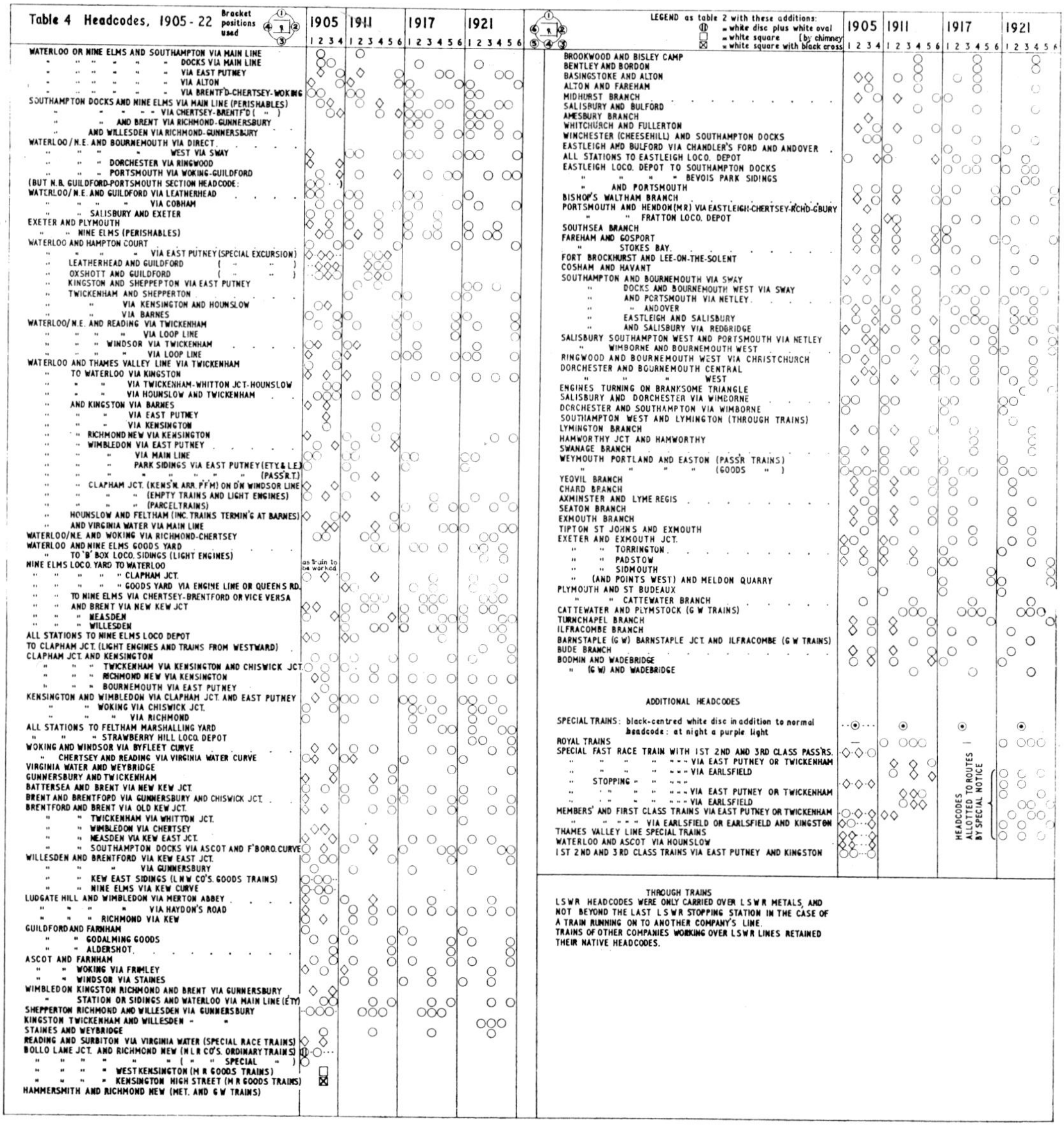

References

1. L S W R, *Rules and Regulations*, Dec. 1847, p. 37.
2. L S W R, *Rules and Regulations*, 1st Aug. 1864, pp. 15-17.
3. L S W R, *Appendix to the Book of Rules . . .*, 1st Jan. 1892.
4. L S W R, *Instruction no. 23*, 1st Nov. 1905, pp. 1-9.
5. L S W R, *Appendix to the Book of Rules . . .*, 1st Jan. 1911, pp. 103-110.
6. L S W R, *Alterations and Additions to Appendix to the Book of Rules and Regulations and to the Working Time Tables*, 3rd Dec. 1917, pp. 1-5.
7. L S W R, *Appendix to the Book of Rules . . .*, 25th July 1921, pp. 129-136.
8. MS sheet in notebook of F. E. Box endorsed "copied from list compiled by Herbert C. Clarke (now dec'd.)".